We are not now that strength which in old days moved earth and heaven, that which we are, we are.'

'Ulysses' - *Alfred Lord Tennyson.*

©Pete Shakespear 2017

<u>Different Roads</u>

Enter a clown, he stands in the spotlight.

INTRODUCTION

ACT ONE

SCENE ONE

SCENE TWO

SCENE THREE

SCENE FOUR

SCENE FIVE

SCENE SIX

ACT TWO

The spotlight fades, the clown quietly exits.

Introduction

After listening to my musings for many years, my son encouraged me to put pen to paper and tell what is perhaps a unique account of life in show business during the 1970's and 80's wherein I had the privilege of working as a lowly jobbing musician. I don't think I've met another musician who over the years played such diverse music as I did, I mean, moving from playing guitar in a soul and reggae band and then plying my trade in the folk and blues clubs both here in the U.K. and Europe. Looking back it would appear to be a strange path to follow, different roads indeed.

This story is not a kiss and tell, what goes on between consenting adults is up to them and should always remain private. It is no secret that musicians have always been a bit racy and I certainly wouldn't want to embarrass anyone, no, it's a series of recollections of musicians, bands, situations, fans and venues that have passed my way over the years, and I hope that you will find the stories amusing and entertaining.

To be honest I have put some of these memories away for years for two reasons. Firstly I hate, and I do mean hate, growing older, and to re-live some of the events is painful, and secondly, I never thought anyone would be interested in my life. I have always viewed myself as of no account; surely all guitar players from unknown little towns have done what I did - now I know that it was not so.

A lot of the young folk in my school and around the village where I grew up played an instrument for a time, their interest most likely aroused due to the explosion of talent coming out of cities like Liverpool, the music coming from the continent of America, and not forgetting television, when for the first time we could see our favourites, not just hear them.

Many soon got bored with the idea of practising for hours and the newly found enthusiasm for music suddenly waned. Being no longer the topic of conversation, the unwanted instrument was often recognized in a second hand shop. Other interests, mainly girls, came along and with it the inevitable settling down. Eventually, the concern for mortgages and job security took over and reality set in for most of the lads, but I was a hopeless dreamer.

Old pals from those days are now beginning to ask me what it was really like as a white musician, in a black band, performing gigs in primarily a black culture and playing music, which was then classed as slightly underground and risqué, and how come that I then made the transition to folk and blues.

Not many people who came to the folk clubs knew of my previous background. Whilst browsing the net some months ago I came across a headline, 'Whatever happened to Pete Shakespear?' well now, I'll tell you, I guess that this is as good a time as any to relate my story.

As I began to reminisce I didn't realise just how the years had evaporated and how I would miss some of the people who used to be in the industry and the clubs where we used to perform.

It started me off delving through a box of memories; I guess we all have something of that sort somewhere in the house. Most of the pictures, posters and autographs are from my own personal collection. I don't know why I collected them, or indeed why I kept them, but it's just as well, I suppose. I was just proud to be achieving something in my life, and it was exciting to think that I may be breaking out from the ordinary daily existence which I felt was the lot of most of the people around me.

I can honestly say that over the years, I have had the wonderful privilege of knowing, meeting and working with, some of the finest talented human beings ever to be put on earth in what I think was one of the most exciting times in popular music. Sadly, but inevitably, I have met some of the biggest shitehawks too!

Nearly everybody who is interested in the history of 1970's and 80's music will have come across the acts that I mention, but I wanted to tell my story from the point of view of an ordinary guitar player, working the night clubs around Britain. Crossing over from the world of night clubs, and into the folk and blues music scene, certainly made for variety and good conversation.

My story may help to show that it was not all glamour - far from it! When an artiste appears on stage and steps into the footlights, the audience could imagine that perhaps show business people live in fabulous houses, drink the finest wine and dine at the best restaurants, for some no doubt that may be true, but for ordinary working musicians it's a gruelling life on the road and sometimes with very little reward.

When you consider that a night club show might begin at around eleven or twelve o'clock and finish in the early hours, add to this the time spent travelling to and from the gig, then you would be hard put to make it to bed for six in the morning (but it's awful having to get out of a warm bed to go home!) It was difficult to hold down a regular job, working in a factory for instance. You couldn't come home around six on a Monday morning and then be at work for eight, something had to go.

The folk clubs in England were usually done and dusted by eleven, but in Europe they could finish at almost any hour, mostly when the last punters left the club. No wonder that a lot of blues singers developed powerful and deep voices, it became like a muscle, the more it was exercised the stronger it became and in a lot of smaller clubs there was no P.A. so one had to learn to project the voice.

To help make a musical education more complete I would urge anyone to follow up on the names mentioned herein, and track down the songs. As a unique generation of humans we have never really, until now, been able to gather so much information and have it at our fingertips. We have a wonderful tool available to us called the Internet, used to right effect, it can help us embark on a never to be forgotten journey of discovering really talented people, ordinary boys and girls who became extraordinary. Do a bit of research and I am sure you will begin to get a taste and flavour of a fabulous age of talent.

It may be that if some of the same young people tried to break out today, they would never be heard, because of the changes in the modern music industry, and the lack of more modest venues where one can begin to learn the trade.

No doubt as you read on, you too will find yourself remembering, and maybe in some small way I can be of encouragement to other fellow life travellers.

If we aim higher we may not fully attain our goal, but if we can reach up and stretch ourselves we will achieve more than we would have expected to, and surely have a good time enjoying our achievements.

Money isn't always the goal, although it makes life a lot easier and more pleasant, it's friendships that are the real and lasting thing, and you cannot buy true friendship, and I did make some good friends along the way.

For the most part my musical journey has been a happy one, as I will attempt to show, but it's also been tinged with tragedy and sadness, part of the rich tapestry of life we all weave, but let's hope that we never lose our sense of proportion and the ability to have a laugh, and as an old sea dog friend of mine, Don Frater, used to sing, always remember, 'Life is just a bowl of cherries ....'

So, that's my introduction over.

Are you sitting comfortably? Then I'll begin.

ACT 1

Scene I

I guess we all have to start somewhere

I was born at 1951 in my grandparents house situated on the border between Willenhall and Wednesfield in the industrial Midlands of England. We lived with them at their house until I was about four. Granddad had been severely wounded in the First World War and there were times when he needed understanding and had to be cared for by my grandma.

During that time I remember what a wonderful woman my grandmother was and some of the expressions she used to use, leading in time to the firing of my imagination. She would take me into a back bedroom, which overlooked the fields, to share with me views over swaying corn. There were no other houses as far as the eye could see, nothing except for the main road that ran from Wednesfield to the hamlet of Bloxwich away in the distance.

There was a fallen tree in a nearby field that she tried to convince me was a dead cow! Once, when I wanted a goldfish, she peeled an orange, put the peel in a bowl of water and swished it round with a stick, she tried for all the world to kid me that it was a real goldfish! At night one could see the twinkling street lights of the road away off and the glow of the buses moving slowly along. She used to tell me,

'That's the lights of the world my lad!'

Now all you can see are thousands of houses, gone are the cornfields and the wonderful star shine of those blackened skies.

On bonfire night she would take me outside to see the rockets and hear the bangs, she called the sounds 'backerappers', a Birmingham expression, but it was also the name of the sound that the soldiers used for the noise of the guns on the Western Front. Dear old granddad was never around on bonfire night, I later found out why. He thought the world of my grandma, and died within a year of her passing away, he couldn't live without her, my father said that he had died of a broken heart.

She was a special lady, she could entertain a child, but always maintained a deep insight into life. It's probably from her that I get my storytelling characteristics, but it's true to say that other members of the family could spin a yarn too. My uncle Tom Birch, a smashing man married to my father's sister Annie, once made me a little scooter. He used to work as an Erk in the RAF during the war and he told me he had made it out of a Spitfire wing!!! One summer my other grandfather, Bill Shirley, made us children's spades to dig in the sandpit. He told us they had been made from the metal in the Queen Mary!

It was one misty autumn night when we all, (father, mother, sister, and my brother still a small baby in the pram) did a moonlight flit to a terraced property, about a mile further into the village, not far from the park. I recall a community air raid shelter left over from the war still on the corner of the lane, and the yellow glow on the pavement of the gas street lighting. A couple of years later my other sister was born here.

The village as it was known locally, was situated on the outskirts of the 'Black Country' of the West Midlands. At that time it was mostly surrounded by a patchwork of golden cornfields and dairy farms. The village was ready for expansion due to the overspill from other towns nearby and was beginning to melt together with Willenhall to the South and Wolverhampton to the West and would soon be swallowed up. There were several working farms within the village, it was still in parts very rural. My cousin Tommy was a groom at a nearby stable, where he looked after the horses which were used to pull the drays carrying milk and bread. I remember even a thatched cottage, wherein supposedly lived a witch. Well she wasn't really, it was a very old lady who came to the window to occasionally watch the children playing in the brook on their way home from school, perhaps seeking out tadpoles or watching a lollipop stick sail away with the gently flowing water. The girls used to run away screaming at the sight of her!

I wonder now who she was and how she must have felt.

Today, older locals still refer to it as 'the village,' but I doubt if many now remember how it used to be. The row of houses where we lived was occupied mostly by workers employed by the engineering factories, locksmiths and chainmakers that made the area world famous. It was christened 'The Black Country' because of the colour of the sky, and the grimy buildings made dirty by the amount of chimney emissions being belched out. We lived on the outskirts, and for now could still see a bit of green landscape.

There is a certain acrid smell in industrial towns, particularly where steel is produced. We had many steel producers nearby, Stuart and Lloyds, Round Oak and Hickman's to mention a few. There was a constant hum in the air of human activity, the noise and smells of 'metal bashing' as we used to call it, drifted over the village all hours from the manufacturing plants around the district. The sounds of steam trains could be heard carried on the wind, as they shunted the myriad of metal things about the many large goods yards and railway sidings situated around the town. Their whistles yelping as the little trains laboured night and day to push the trucks into the correct siding to meet the designated freight train and be shipped all over the country, and the world. The cacophony of noise would be heard twenty four hours a day, chuff, chuff, chuff, clang as the buffers met, whissstll, and the slow puff, puff, as a larger engine toiled to gather speed and carry its cargo to some unknown destination. Exactly on time an express train would clatter through on the main line. Other sounds of manufacturing filled the air, the metallic 'clang' as another weld-less steel tube hit the workshop floor and the thump of heavy drop forge hammers pounded; all this noise of human activity only ceasing for a shift change, or a national holiday such as Christmas, or the annual two week works shutdown in August, and of course Sunday, the day of rest.

At different times of the day and night, the sad wailing sounds of many factory sirens, or 'bulls' as they were known, would float across the town. Some were the same ones as had been used in the war to announce the Germans were about to drop in for an air raid, or to sing the all-clear. The melancholy moan would summon the workers to rise and prepare for another chance to earn their daily bread. They would be sounded again to indicate that it was ten minutes to the hour and then again on the hour, reminding them that they should be at work. Hurry, don't be late or you will be 'quartered,' that meant that if you were one minute late you would lose fifteen minutes pay! The wailing went on day and night, either to indicate the times of shift changeover, clocking on time and 'knock off,' or finishing time. Sunday morning was quiet, the peace broken only by a peal of church bells or the sound of a bugle as the boy's brigade marched around the village. At evensong a lonely bell tolled to call the faithful to meet with God, offering them solace from their labours. The midday aromas of Sunday lunch being cooked and shared by families would waft through the streets, a tradition now alas in the past, as society has changed so much.

We used to listen to the radio in those days; I only knew one kid whose family had a television, apart from Mr Ball, our next door neighbour. We laughed at the humour of 'Julian and Sandy' of 'Round the Horn' fame, but for the most part couldn't understand some of the expressions and double entendre they used, but it was funny. During the evening my parents used to listen to a programme called 'Sing Something Simple,' so depressing! - a choir and an accordion, jeeezzzz!!

Monday began a normal working week, most people started their labours around 8am, but the large manufacturing plants had shift systems that would be something like 6am till 2pm, then 2pm till 10pm, followed by the night shift of 10pm till 6am, but not all the factories followed this regime. Armies of men would be seen cycling to, or returning from work, come rain or shine, whatever the season, always the same.

The general apparel of the working men in those days comprised of flat caps, bicycle clips and an ex-army haversack containing a thermos flask and sandwiches. Morning and evening and during shift change over, the village and surrounding streets would become a hive of activity, and because of men on bicycles, trolley buses, heavy lorries, horse and carts all jostling with a mass of humanity and all moving at the same time; the village would come to a grinding halt and travel to and from work would be slow.

Those lucky enough to be employed on the 'staff' of a company didn't start work until 9am and a bit of a snobby attitude was in the air as they made their way to the office in suit and tie; some of them thought they were a 'cut above' the men who had to get their hands dirty to earn their pay. The early episodes of 'The Likely Lads' epitomises this time of social change perfectly.

The general pastime for most of the working men was either gardening or keeping pigeons. At weekends, little clouds of 'tumblers' or 'rollers' would be seen fluttering in the air, a 'homer' would whistle over the houses watched eagerly by flat capped 'fanciers' as they rattled tins of corn to attract them into landing back to the loft. Others would content themselves by attempting to grow a prize bloom, or to simply provide the family vegetables for the week.

A lot of goods and commodities were still delivered around the houses by horse drawn dray. The coalman, the village baker, milkman and the scrap metal collector would all use a horse and some type of cart from which to conduct their daily business. When one of these tradesmen was seen in the street, it would cause the inevitable scramble to find a bucket and shovel to collect the deposited horse manure from the road, so that it could be used as fertiliser for the vegetable patch.

There used to be a rag and bone man who went around the village using a horse and cart to ply his trade. He attracted attention by blowing a bugle and shouting, 'Any old rags?' His cries echoed around the streets providing ample time to sort out any items that were to be given in exchange for a few coppers, or a goldfish in a water filled plastic bag! The crafty old chap used to make regular visits during school holidays, knowing that the kids were at home. He knew that we were a bit gullible and would bring him almost anything to be given a 'pet.' Some kids were known to have received a good belting for giving the tatter their dad's best trousers or shirt! I have seen many a mom hurtling off around the street, holding at arm's length a goldfish in a plastic bag, attempting to retrieve some precious item of clothing. People had to be resourceful and tried to eke out as much use from clothing and any other material possessions as they could. Make do and mend was the norm in most families.

Some ladies took in washing for other women who had found a job in the factory, perhaps on an assembly line. Many children had a newspaper round, others ran errands and were allowed to 'keep the change' if it was a spare halfpenny or the odd 'coppers.' (*A copper was the old name for a penny*).

Life wasn't all bad, we tried to make use of every opportunity to have a bit of fun. The days approaching Bonfire

Night were a time of dressing up for the custom of 'Penny for the Guy' when, to be honest, we went begging, under the cover of asking for money for poor old Guy Fawkes. In reality, the money was spent as quickly as we received it, in the corner shop, on sweets or a comic. You may remember that an effigy of the poor bugger Guy was made from old clothes stuffed with straw, later to be burned on the bonfire.

I recall one misty November evening when a little gang of us assembled on the corner of the street with a girl called Meggy posing as Guy Fawkes. We must have resembled 'The Perishers' - still my favourite cartoon series. Meggy was dressed in some old trousers and an oversized cardigan, with an old ladies purple hat with faded dried flowers around the rim, perched on her head. On her face she had a papier-mâché mask of Guy and straw and paper stuffed into the neck and arms of her clothing. She was lying in an old pram, which had been taken from some unsuspecting parent. Being a tall girl, she didn't really fit the pram properly and her legs were dangling down the sides of it, but she did her best to appear 'dead.' Trying not to move, she lay there motionless, as we took turns in the fading light to push the 'corpse' around the village streets. All went well until at a bus stop we approached a miserable old sod who, when we asked,

'Penny for the guy mister?' promptly began to holler,
'That guy just moved!'

'No it didn't!' we all exclaimed.

As he began to shout even louder, attempting to attract attention, Meggy lost her nerve and shot out of the pram causing us all to bolt. There was straw and paper flapping in all directions and we disappeared down alleyways as if we were the ones about to be thrown on to the bonfire! The empty, lightened, panicked pram careered down a short incline and overturned in someone's front garden, wheels and clumps of turf were hurled into the misty night air. The remains of the pram were retrieved later that evening when we saw that the daft sod had caught his bus and was gone. The boys reckoned that what was untwisted would make a good soap box racer. Somebody must have received a sound thrashing after having to own up to taking the pram without permission and then eventually, when returning home empty handed, having to admit that the pram was smashed up and ruined.

The ubiquitous pram was not only used to transport babies, but also snotty kids to school and back. They also served to carry the shopping from the village and fetch small bags of coal directly off the barges moored at the canal wharf, if, as was often the case, one could not afford to have a full horse drawn delivery from Mr Grosvenor the local coal merchant. We would lean over the canal bridge and listen to the pud, pud, pud sound of the Bolinder engine and watch the whisp of blue smoke curl away on the wind, as a barge pulling 'butties' filled with coal, snaked up the canal. The gaily decorated boats made their way to the factory wharves, their hard won cargo then discharged into the boiler rooms that powered the nations industry. The canals and barges were still part of working life, but their use was beginning to decline.

During the weeks leading up to Bonfire Night the local boys would scour the area for anything to build the fire, including chopping down perfectly good small shrubs and trees, much to the consternation of gardeners, and woe betide anyone who didn't hide wood in all its forms, orange boxes, rabbit hutches and the like. If it would burn it was fair game! Some years it was a competition to see which family or street would have the biggest fire! There was a rumour that one little girl only discovered, too late, that her dolls house had contributed to the delightful flames, when she noticed little twisted hinges and melted blobs of plastic in the embers of a bonfire the next morning.

Summer school holidays were a mixture of boredom and mischief. Activities such as setting alight to the long grass in the alleyway alongside the park using the glue from a bicycle puncture repair kit, or placing a corrugated sheet from an old air raid shelter across the path to divide it. The kids would take sides and hurl stones and broken bricks at each other for fun; peals of laughter filled the air as the missiles clanged off the iron, until somebody caught a good 'un and blood was spilt, then everyone scattered.

The annual funfair and carnival held in the park was the highlight of the year. Apart from rides like the 'Waltzer,' 'Octopus' and the 'Dodgem' cars, we would delight to a display of military vehicles, fire engine drills and a civil defence simulated rescue, where a casualty was saved from a very high scaffolding tower; so exciting to us kids. We never paid to gain entrance. Being poor meant that we were thin and could slip between the iron railings, albeit with some help from a couple of the older boys who would bend the bars, making them a bit wider and we always managed to evade the beady eye of the fairground boss. In little gangs we hung around the attractions that flew the giggling people around and around and into the air, because someone always dropped a few coins from their pockets as they whizzed round in circles. We scooped them up as soon as we spotted them hitting the ground. The big pennies were immediately slotted into a machine with a handle that was turned by hand.

The intriguing name of the machine was, 'What the Butler Saw,' and was the main attraction for us boys. Each took it in turn to peek into the little funnel which lit up the flickering world of naughty, forbidden delights contained therein; pictures that we hoped would reveal the answer to our curiosity. The damn machine always ran out of money just as the maid was about to reveal all! We fell for it every time, hoping that the next penny would bring us better luck, but no matter how quickly or slowly we turned the handle, the results were always the same - no titty!!

The house where we lived was an austere, cold, middle of a terrace property, three up, two down, outside coalhouse and privy, and sad to say, the place was haunted! I suppose that little kids don't really understand why certain things happen; they may just feel uneasy and that something is not right. In the house there was always an air of being watched, particularly at the top of the stairs. Often items would drop off the table and onto the floor for no apparent reason. Doors would either open slowly or be flung open aggressively. Furniture would tremble, causing its handles to rattle. The sound of a metallic object falling onto a concrete floor would shock the house in the middle of the night. What on earth this sound was, I have never been able to find out; some might say that it was the house moving due to the activity of perhaps mining or heavy engineering, but the factories were some miles away and combined with other strange and unexplained events I think that a poltergeist was present in the property. People say that goings on like this are just the product of a child's imagination, but I beg to differ. On several occasions I awoke during the night with an uneasy feeling of being watched, only to find a grey, smoke-like apparition standing staring at me. For a few seconds I would stare back into the empty eye sockets thinking that it may be my mother, she having perhaps entered the room unbeknown to me whilst I was sleeping. Once it dawned on me that I could see right through the ghostly apparition to the wall beyond, I would immediately throw the bedclothes over my head. With my heart almost jumping out of my chest, a sudden extreme cold would envelop the room and my hair would literally stand on end. Under the bedclothes I would stay until daylight broke the spell.

There was an amusing incident which occurred many years later, although it was not amusing at the time! I had just returned home after a gig at around 2am in the morning. Unable to sleep, having not yet relaxed from the night's activities, I decided to re-string and polish my guitar ready for the next performance. As I sat in the 'front room' happily polishing away with my yellow duster, the drawn floor to ceiling curtains began to move. Movement began slowly at first, flapping more vigorously as my attention was becoming fully engaged. Very afraid, I stood up. I had had enough of being frightened by a 'ghost' and summoned all my strength to whimper the words,

'What do you want?'

'Who are you?'

The movements were getting more exaggerated; I stepped toward the curtains, fists clenched.

'Who are you?' I began to demand.

'What do you want of me?'

Truth to tell, fear coursed through my veins, but in some situations you reach a point when it's me or him, or it! I had to face the phenomena! As I reached out to fling open the curtains, by now flapping away madly, our little dog Paddy stepped out, his tail wagging in excited greeting. It was his wagging tail that had been moving the curtains! He must have heard me enter the house and had been sleeping in a warm spot between the wall and the curtain. He lived to a ripe old age, eighteen, but I am afraid that he and I nearly didn't live to tell the tale that night. I go cold when I think of that house even now. To this day I will not watch horror movies and I will have nothing at all to do with the occult.

Many years ago some friends of mine were holding a séance using an Ouija board, back in the days when it was thought of as entertainment to consult them. They posed it the question, 'What is the secret of life?' The answer came back 'H7' repeatedly. They asked me if I knew what H7 was. I am afraid I didn't, and neither did the foolish enquirers. One of them visited a local library to research the question and reported back that he'd discovered that H7 was an amino acid, without which cells do not move correctly, or something like that. I am afraid that that was enough for me to know, I firmly believe that there are more things out there than we know about in this world. A lot of people think that dabbling into such things is just harmless fun, but after my childhood spent living at that house, it is not a view I share.

A couple of years ago I had cause to pass through what was 'the village' and was surprised to see how it had been built up, people, cars and housing estates everywhere. Seeing the massive development reminded me of a comment made by a dear friend of mine, Brian Wedge, alas no longer with us. Brian was 94 years of age and I respectfully asked him one day what it was like to be 94. His reply I now understand, it was,

'I am still 25 in my head Pete, but I look around and

wonder, where did all these people come from?'

I attended a little infant's school within walking distance of my home, but didn't progress very well - read on and you will probably find out why. I recently found an old school report which stated simply, 'Peter is a bit slow.' They didn't pull their punches in those days and along with many working class kids, it appeared that I was beaten before I started! As part of the government's plan to feed the nation after the war, the children were allowed a small bottle of full fat milk each day; sickly smelling in summer, and icy cold in winter. In class the cheesy smell of milk clung to you all day after the morning break.

Sometimes on winter days the silver metallic lid would be forced up by an icicle formed in the bottle by the harsh cold, or in the spring the lids had holes pecked in them where the birds had had first go at the contents. But, sad to tell, there was always some poor sod fainting during morning assembly through lack of food.

I hated the silliness of the cane which could be dished out if you were a minute late for school, or you got your sums wrong; apparently it was viewed as medicine in order to 'wake us up' or teach us discipline. I was caned once for passing wind during the school orchestra practise, bastards! I was farting in tune and on the beat!!!

Some of the teachers seemed to look with disdain on us poor buggers, whilst appearing to prefer the company of the local doctor's son or the undertaker's lad or the fireman's boy.

The schools used to have a regular visit from the 'nit nurse' or health visitor. I remember once that we had to have a hearing test. The class was duly lined up in the headmaster's office, now doubling as a surgery. All I saw was that the lad in front of me, Victor Robinson, had a set of headphones placed on his head and for all intents and purposes was just standing there in front of the headmaster's desk repeating the word, 'Yes.'

When it came to my turn and the headphones were put on my head, I too just stood there saying,

'Yes,' 'Yes,'.......until I noticed the giggling nurse; me being a thick bastard hadn't seen the machine on the desk. I didn't clock that she had to press keys on it so that different frequencies of sound could be used to test the efficiency of our hearing. I still tell that story at dinner parties, much to the amusement of my guests! Ooh, what was I like! It happened again when we were to be inspected for verrucas; I thought they said we were going in for Bazookas, I ran away screaming thinking they were going to blow our feet off!

In winter, the days seemed dark and foggy; a yellow fog that would enter a room if you left the door or a window open long enough. The sulphurous smell of the fog from the myriad of coal fires and the metallic smell of manufacturing combined for the most part to make the dark nights depressing, and gloominess seemed to pervade our lives. When the fog was really bad the buses stopped running and everything ground to a halt leaving a strange eerie quiet. The winters too could be harsh and walking to school in snow up to the knees meant chill-blains, cold sores and chapped legs. I can still recall the smell of wintergreen.

The future prospects held out to us from the secondary modern school I attended were not much better, although I did well at art and was advised to further my studies at Art College. No chance. On leaving school you couldn't go home without a job, and art was not considered a proper job! I learned years later, that the government spend on children who had passed the eleven plus exam and who had made it into a Grammar school, was almost twice the amount spent on those who it appeared were already condemned to life as losers. When it came time to see the careers master he simply said,

'I think we will put you down for engineering.'

That was it, I was vomited forth from school and into a factory.

The introduction to the world of work was a noisy workshop. Spinning belts from shafts high above the factory floor powered rows of drilling machines and lathes producing brass parts for valves. I didn't seem to be learning much and it wasn't long before I resented being used as cheap labour working one of these antiquated pieces of machinery.

It came to a head one day when I was reprimanded for grabbing a mouthy storekeeper by the throat and pulling him through the little window opening in the door of the stores. I pulled so hard that he became firmly wedged up to his waist in the hole, his legs were flapping wildly and his face turned blue! This was much to the delight of the tool makers who began banging hammers and spanners on their benches and cheering. Apparently the little pratt had had it coming for a while.

Back then the older men used to take great delight in sending inexperienced and 'green' newcomers off to the stores to ask for a 'long stand' or a 'left-handed spanner,' but this storeman, miserable old sod, seemed to think that it was done at his expense, not the silly sap waiting for hours to receive the 'long stand!' I was so gullible that I fell for it every time! After a few choice words with the shitbag named Haywood, who was the Personnel officer, I told him to put his job up his arse and I left. I was eventually taken on as an apprentice toolmaker at a company owned by an ex-army officer.

Major Maley was a gentleman and made it a point to speak to all the workforce every morning, including me, the lowly new boy. A lesson in management I have never forgotten.

As an apprentice I was allowed one day each week to attend engineering college. At the college one of my instructors, Mr Horton, would say I was, 'a square peg in a round hole.' I couldn't wait to break away. The chaps in the tool room had a saying, whenever I questioned them about their lives, that 'You won't beat the system.' The tool-room blokes, Jack Townsend, Larry Stevens, Les Cowley and old Heric Willis were fine men and really I guess, couldn't understand why I was so restless.

Most of the large factories had a works canteen which provided regular evening entertainment throughout the week and at weekends for the employees and their families.

Monday night was usually 'free and easy,' where an organist and drummer played in the background while the audience had a quiet drink. At midweek there was usually a talent competition. They called it a 'shop window' where entertainment secretaries from other clubs in the area attended to review any new acts, and hopefully offer them a booking at their own venue. Saturday was dance night with a group or small combo performing all types of music from pop to ballroom. Sunday lunchtime was for men only, this meant beer, dirty comedians and striptease! The Christmas and New Year's Eve shows could be quite lavish affairs, with tickets going on sale months before, and from a performer's point of view were the best paying gigs of the year.

During nearly all these entertainment shows, the time between the 'turns' was interspersed with several games of Bingo. When a game was being played you couldn't even whisper before someone 'hushed' you or gave you a dirty look. They took it really seriously. Eyes down look in! Two houses and a flier, with the winning prize of a fiver, what an existence! The caller usually sat on the stage next to a machine which had air blowing through it to agitate and mix up numbered coloured balls. He picked out a ball and then called out the number accompanied by a catchy phrase like clickety click number 66, or something like that, anyway, if the number was on your ticket you had to cross the number off. The first person to tick off all the selected numbers won, and called out 'house!' or 'line!' if they had the first line completed. A 'flyer' was a quick game played for a prize usually given by the management. (I thought that the game had died out but lately there seems to be a resurgence). In some clubs there really was an announcement that the meat pies were ready!

Most of the entertainment secretaries, who had specific responsibility for booking the performers, were ordinary men working in the factory by day, but who could behave like gods and become little Hitlers during the evening at the club. They received power from the Holy Spirit of the Committee to dictate their orders, usually in a very surly manner, to the acts appearing at the club who put on a show for them; sometimes almost viewing them as slaves.

I find it amazing that when you give some very ordinary people a measure of responsibility it can make them think they are invincible, and they begin to bully others; it happens in all walks of life. If it transpired that you offended one of these awful little people, you could face being banned from their club 'sine die,' without a day, or for life! Heaven forbid that the name of the act and petty misdemeanour was published in the monthly club-land magazine, you had had it! A change of name for the act and not working that club again for a year or so would usually suffice, hoping that you were not recognised by the club secretary if he saw you at another venue. Thankfully, not all were like it, but a lot were.

Due to the many working men's clubs, pubs, Labour, Conservative and Liberal clubs, and factory canteens, there were plenty of regular bookings to be had for any bunch of young people who had the tenacity to put a show together.

Nearly all pubs had a piano, a throwback to earlier days when people provided their own entertainment. If you were feeling competent enough, the landlord would let you use it for a sing song on a Saturday night; this type of piano playing was not too demanding and as the evening wore on most of the clientele were in a world of their own anyway. It helped many a young budding musician to develop the qualities of an entertainer.

There was also a thriving ballroom and university circuit and an emerging night club scene. This created ample opportunity to build a business in the industry if you worked at it hard enough. The night club and concert scene was the league that most bands aspired to, or if you were in a pop band a summer season in one of the holiday camps would be a goal and many television entertainers started their careers in this way.

I can only ever remember performing at a couple of working men's clubs when they had a show during mid week, although we picked up plenty of work for the special occasions such as Christmas and New Year's Eve. I didn't like performing at these clubs, I found a lot of the secretaries small minded and petty.

Also, stopping every hour for a Bingo session was not my idea of being in show business, although a lot of my fellow musicians relied on them for their living, particularly the organ and drum duos. The really successful organists got to perform on the radio, 'The Organist Entertains,' and could command a good fee for a show. I remember working in the studio once with a great organist, Brian Sharp who was particularly highly regarded in the clubs. Brian's career spanned some 50 years, but I learned that he had died aged 78 in January of 2016. He will be sadly missed.

Some young musicians, whilst still holding down a regular job, could make more money playing in a band at weekends than their weekly wages.

Not many though could keep the two going, and sooner or later came the inevitable choice, whether to stay in the factory or office or take the chance and see if fame really did beckon. I guess that it was worth taking the chance, you are only young once.

During the years emerging from the horrors of the Second World War, there was nearly full employment, and working men had had enough of the class system and began to find subservience unacceptable. If a man was bored with his job or found a better paying employer, he could resign at 10 o'clock and find a new position by midday, not as now, where you are glad to have a job at any price - and don't employers know it! The idea of job security began to change in the eighties when the government of the day appeared to declare war on the working man and once again we were only too glad to be in employment and had to eat a lot of humble pie.

I once worked with a man who had a very skilled job in the factory. He earned good money. On Saturdays he had a market stall from where he sold the children's toys which he had made in his garage, such as steam engines made from cocoa tins; you pulled them along on a piece of string. He also made wooden ducks; on the wheels were little rubber feet made from old bicycle inner tubes which flapped as they went round. At Christmas he sold other items around the factory, stuff he would get to order from a wholesaler. At the weekend he went out performing as a dirty comedian and was well paid for his idea of comedy. Unfortunately he was the meanest man I ever met. He came to work on a moped or, if it rained, he appeared driving an old Hillman Minx, both had no tax or insurance; I think he would have put any miser to shame! My feeling was that this type of performer, naughty Bert Baker, was at the tackier end of show business.

There were always ones that posed as agents who hung around the stages and preyed on the vulnerable. Mister 10% would always try to convince you that he knew so and so and could guarantee that you would turn pro within a year, provided of course that you crossed his palm with silver. Some were very professional, others were charlatans and it was usually too late by the time you had discovered what the small print in the contract really meant and to then realise your money was not forthcoming. A decent agent would probably be a member of a recognised body, and with the use of the internet, information is more freely available about the meaning of words used in contracts; and through social media it is easier to find the real reputation of the agent or the company they represent.

Pick any street and there would be quite a few kids who played an instrument. Within a very short radius of where I lived I knew ones that played saxophone, trumpet, bass guitar, and there were at least two drummers. In my class at school there were several really good guitar players. We swopped chord sequences and riffs; and met at each other's houses to busk together. You learn much more when hanging out with other like minded musicians and also encourage one another. Even the school had its own 'beat group' which performed at the end of term leaving parties. As I recall, they weren't much good, but they delighted in their small time fame.

Music was everywhere and there was a feeling that anyone could 'make it' if they were tenacious and had talent or could find a 'gimmick.' Multiply this creativity up on a national scale and it just shows the pool of very talented young people that were around.

Not every musician took it as far as we did. Most found a girlfriend and settled down, and then a lot of them were given the ultimatum: me or music, which? One band I heard of were accepted to appear on a television show called 'Opportunity Knocks' fronted by Hughie Green. One of the young guitarists in the band was given the 'ultimatum' and decided to pull out. Who knows where it would have led, and all because our 'little missy' did not want her boyfriend to become famous or go anywhere without her. Incidentally, the band quickly took on a replacement guitarist and went on to do well in the show, and they did eventually turn pro!

There were a lot of talented acts that passed through the studios of that show, and some have become national treasures. Most artistes that appeared on the programme used it as a publicity vehicle and worked for many years afterward. The 'Reason Why' was asked to take part in the show at one time, but due to commitments could not make it, anyway several of the members of the band considered that it was not the right vehicle, oh well!

At a young age I almost found myself in the 'ultimatum' position and sadly I had to call a halt to the relationship. It was all getting a bit too serious and tense for me. I know the experience was painful and probably appeared to be a shitty trick by onlookers, however I knew that the only way out of poverty for me was to try to build a future in show business; there was no future for me in a factory. I would not accept being dictated to or blackmailed by anyone, I had to let my head rule my heart, I am still a bit like that now. For me, waiting and not settling for the first romance paid off in the sense that eventually I found someone who was not jealous of the 'harsh mistress' called show business, after all, we hoped it would put bread on the table and bring us happy times. Sometimes it did, but often it didn't.

As I began to move around in the music scene it was plain to see that there were a lot of unhappy relationships among the married musicians I was getting to know. Long faced wives would reluctantly wave off their 'would be star' as he climbed into the band van to be off to a gig, perhaps leaving her lonely, jealous and suspicious as to what he may get up to. I would notice how a bloke's face would light up when he saw who was waiting for him at the stage door, and you had to remember ladies' names pretty quickly in case you blurted out the wrong name in front of the wrong girl! A different girl at every gig; I was a naive seventeen year old and for the most part kept my mouth shut.

Show business wives who stick to their man are really special. It always seems that the opposite sex are attracted to someone with a bit of something about them. They then proceed to try to change all of that when they think they have got their hooks into them. I suppose that is the meaning of the saying, 'Aisle, altar, hymn' - I'll alter him!

How times have changed though; the opportunities to perform that we then had have diminished and many, many venues have now disappeared; the Plaza's, Locarno's, Scala Ballrooms and many dancehalls, along with the factories and the working men's clubs - all gone. It must be hard to learn the trade now. The price of new, professional, musical equipment has made it difficult for young ones to afford to even start, without a lot of help from the bank of 'Mom and Dad.' With very few venues left, gaining the experience and the confidence to pick up an instrument and entertain in a good old fashioned clean way are slowly disappearing, but perhaps I'm getting a bit long in the tooth; at least the folk scene will give someone a chance if they are willing to put themselves in front of an audience. Even here though, I get a little disillusioned when I hear about a performer whose first gig is a festival appearance, what's that about! These gigs were usually reserved for time served professionals who could bring in an audience!

I also find it strange when you consider that a playable second hand guitar might have cost a fiver from a junk shop, now the same type of instrument is several hundreds of pounds. I heard recently that a pal of mine sold his original 1960's Fender Stratocaster for the price of a small motor car! Of course there was always the kid whose parents bought their 'little star' the very best straight off, but sadly it was very rare that these were the really gifted ones.

This generation appears to be left with stage school people, or wannabee dreamers singing to a hair brush in a mirror, possibly not their fault entirely; blame the fame culture and cheap reality television entertainment. Witness the endless queues to audition for these shows, only to be put at the mercy of people who are quite often nothing more than using young ones with the desperation for fame, in order to make a programme. Sadly, many appear to think they are stars even before they have achieved anything! I also find it amazing how narked some of them can get when you won't listen to their dirges or compliment them on their wonderful 'talent.'

Parents too can push their little angels to be precocious, some attempting to re-live their lives through their children. I knew a policeman's son who, at the age of twelve, could reduce his father to tears by his demands, all because they thought that the little pratt was going to be a star organist on the working men's club scene. I have never heard of him since.

One A&R man recently told me that in their desperation to be famous, some silly buggers will promise to do almost anything for a deal. What is it about show business that can reduce perfectly rational human beings to offer to do the most devilish things for fame? If these short sighted hopefuls think that show business folk are rich - although some undoubtedly are - just take a look around, there is many a household name that has been left with very little after a lifetime in the industry.

There were many extremely talented working bands and musicians in the Midlands, and indeed all over the country. Every town had more than one band, plying their trade in an old Commer or Transit van up and down the nation, attempting to make it. Some painted the name of the band on the side of the vehicle for publicity; you couldn't do that now, all your gear would get nicked if 'Mr Opportunist' knew it was a band van.

Your treasured instruments would probably be sold off cheaply in a shady pub somewhere, just so some idiot could put a line of dope up their nose, a plague of our age!!

Many of the musicians moved freely around the different local groups and most knew, or had worked with each other, at some time or another, particularly if the musicians played the same genre of music. The major recording companies were approachable too. You could in those days, if you tried hard enough, get through to the movers and shakers and executives of the industry and find a listening ear; the appetite for new songs was insatiable, but you had to be lucky, not every song or band was signed up.

Many towns had recording studios, McLachlan's in Albrighton and Hollick and Taylor in Birmingham were such ones. These could be hired for a session to cut an acetate demonstration disc, or they could make you a reel to reel tape recording of your work which would then be hawked around London, as I said, often times being heard by someone within the record companies.

When working on stage with a well known writer recently, Ray Froggatt (Ray wrote many wonderful songs including Red Balloon, recorded by The Dave Clark Five), I asked him how he got his start and he said it was, 'Just luck Pete, just luck,' but that is not to take away the fact that he is a really talented professional - but there is a certain amount of luck involved -

unless you happen to have the right contacts! Like most young kids of the time I liked popular music. I thought Billy Fury was the best ballad singer ever and fancied myself being like that - fat chance! Many years later I did manage to get Billy's autograph, one of my most treasured possessions, I'll show you later if you are good.

It was after I had been watching my Auntie Annie's television and seen the Everly Brothers singing 'Wake up little Suzy,' that I wanted to learn to play the guitar, I guess I was about ten years of age.

I recently had the pleasure of meeting Albert Lee, the man responsible for the 1983 reunion concert for the Everly's; Albert performed with them for over twenty years, a great musician!

It was when I was about 11 years of age that I received my first guitar, bought for me as a Christmas present, along with a copy of the book, 'Bert Weedon's Play in a Day.' Play in a day!!! I'm still learning, umpteen odd years later. The first year that I had my guitar I broke my arm in a cycling accident which delayed my progress somewhat, but eventually when the plaster came off, I mastered the tuning method and began to place my fingers on the neck of the guitar and tried to make sounds that made sense. Even after all these years I really am one of the world's worst guitar players, especially now that I don't play regularly, but I still love to plonk a tune or two when the mood takes me.

An early influence on my life was my uncle, John Shirley. Uncle John showed me a few chords on the guitar, but really he was an accomplished harmonica player. He occasionally performed at works concerts and Christmas parties; his harmonica rendering of 'Cherry Pink and Apple Blossom White' was superb. My other grandfather and grandmother, Bill and Mary Shirley, were really proud of 'our John', and rightly so. Granny Shirley's maiden name was Garrity and she took great delight in telling everybody that Freddie Garrity, of Freddie and the Dreamers, was my cousin!

Like most kids learning to play at that time, I tried to work out the chords to Dylan songs, or 'Colours' by Donovan. Trying to change from C to F seemed nigh on impossible, but try G to C, it's even worse; but with patience the sounds began to happen and the buzzing from the strings got less as the strength in my fingers developed. All musicians know the feeling.

One Friday evening after school, me and a chap who was in my class named Dennis Grew, caught the bus a short ride to Willenhall in the West Midlands, to visit a folk club held in a pub called 'The Three Crowns' I think it was, if I remember right. It was Dennis' idea; he was into folk and blues and liked the style of Bert Jansch and John Renbourn and he was becoming an accomplished exponent of that style. Being underage we should not really have been drinking, let alone in the pub! We ordered half a bitter each and hung about sheepishly at the back of the room. The first act to perform was 'The Black Country Three,' they must have been what I now know as the residents, and they performed traditional working chain-makers songs. They were professional and entertaining, but the music was not my cup of tea.

Then they announced that the guest singer was Derek Brimstone. Obviously I had never heard of any of these people, or heard any of the songs before, but as Derek performed we listened spellbound. Now I was introduced to what true musicianship and performing was about. This man stood there in the middle of the room and sang, played and talked to the audience, as if they were all his family; a truly marvellous entertainer. He played guitar and banjo and told travellers' stories, looking for all the world like a teacher wearing, what we described later to our schoolmates as, a 'Beatles' hat. This man was superb; many years later our paths crossed and we performed on the same bill on several occasions, wonderful treasured memories.

About once a week an early evening news programme from the Midlands called ATV Today would have a musical interlude where they invited guest artistes to perform.

Among others this included Roger Whittaker, and The Black Country Three, but the performer who I really wanted to hear was a very youthful Gerry Lockran. More about Gerry later, but suffice to say that Gerry was perhaps the greatest acoustic blues player in the world, and I wanted to play that kind of music. Truth to tell, unfortunately I've never been able to master the style; I simply am not good enough! I also enjoyed listening to the voices of Ray Charles, Sam and Dave, Otis Redding, and Percy Sledge and many other black gospel type singers began to interest me, along with blues players like Robert Johnson.

Musicians in the coastal towns where ships visited and traded with America had a distinct advantage. During their visits to foreign shores, the crews of the ships were exposed to the new popular music and traditional Blues, now taking hold among the younger generation. They were able to obtain recordings of some of the best and bring them back to the U.K. Listen to the early Beatles and Stones recordings; I'm sure you will hear the echoes of Delta Blues influence.

Billy Fury had hits with a lot of covers by a relatively little heard of artiste and wonderful singer called Arthur Alexander. Arthur disappeared into oblivion and became a bus driver. He died virtually unknown and poor; it just isn't fair is it?

Being land locked, and as far as you could be from the sea, in the Midlands, we had to rely on the wireless, particularly radio Luxembourg. The sounds of the music used to reach a high and then fade out in the ether, you had to hear a tune many times before you got the full song and lyrics. If you liked what you heard, it was a case of ordering from a record shop, especially if the act was not in the main stream; but nowadays the internet can provide all that the listener wants, well, very nearly.

On Sunday nights Tom Jones hosted a great show on television; his resident guitarist was Big Jim Sullivan and together with Steve Cropper's style of playing I was inspired to want to play like them. The feeling I got when I heard the beat put out by this type of soul music, together with the sound of the horns of the brass section, made me feel good and stirred my emotions. I wanted to be in a soul band and made up my mind to ditch the acoustic guitar when I could - and go electric! Little did I know that I would eventually come full circle.

By now I had been vomited forth from my Secondary Modern school, still with my head in the clouds - and ended up in a factory as I said, as an apprentice toolmaker. I hated the smell of the machines and the slurry oil and the blackness and noise that surrounded me. The prevailing atmosphere in the factory was that most of the men I worked with had given up hope of anything better, and that I should be glad I had a job. Job stands for 'Just Over Broke!' and I felt that I had been given a bag of dog shit and told to deal with it!

Eventually, with a couple of bob off my father and a bit of saving from my pay packet, I purchased a second hand Hofner Verithin guitar, a bright red one, the nearest to a Gibson 335 I could afford. Today, I would love to get that guitar back. I sold it many years ago when I was on my beam ends; possibly all musicians, when they get older, reminisce about a favourite instrument.

As a side point, as time went on, the blokes in the factory knew I played the guitar and that I was looking to gig out at weekends. One of the men said that if he ever won the pools he would buy me a brand new guitar. Guess what, yes, one Monday morning the telephone in the toolroom rang and he answered it. The receiver was quietly and without fuss replaced on the cradle, he collected his snap bag and walked across the yard to be met by his brother and father who also worked at the factory. They walked out of the gate together and were never seen again. They had won a massive £300,000 on Littlewoods, that's £100,000 each! I never had that new guitar!

Taking the plunge I placed an order for a Selmer 30 watt amp on hire purchase through a company called Bells Musical Instruments; you could send for their catalogue which was advertised in all the newspapers. I wish I had kept a copy of the catalogue, it was a mine of information and photographs of what are now vintage guitars, amps and stuff.

I began to try and learn the riffs and chords to the most wonderful songs that, even to this day, still lift my spirits. It was now a different style of playing to my acoustic guitar. As I could not read a note of music, I played the songs on the record player, and stopped the album track every few minutes to try out what I thought was the correct chord sequence, oh my fingers were sore! It was a triumph to be able to play along through a whole album note for note; you felt part of the band.

How strings have changed too, today they can be very light indeed, or you can make up a set using your own favourite weight, but we unfortunately had to make do with tape wound. (They made tape wound strings to help stop the little squeal as the fingers moved over the fretboard of the guitar.)

Before the tips of my fingers began to callous, I had to burn them by touching them on a hot gas ring to stop the soreness and bleeding blisters! The price of a set of new strings was a bit expensive for an apprentice on four quid a week, so I was taught a trick by a great guitarist, Terry Garvey, who played like Chet Atkins. He showed me how to rejuvenate the strings by boiling them like an egg for three minutes. This would only work temporarily as it made the strings brittle and they would snap after a few days, but it would get you out of trouble if money was tight, although later when the bookings came in, we used a new set of strings for each concert.

The neighbours must have been bored out of their skulls to hear the same tunes constantly stopping and starting, and I must admit I did turn up the record player as high as it would go without distorting the sound, but eventually I began to develop a repertoire of soul songs.

On Saturday mornings, along with a couple of friends,

Robert Hutton and Dennis Grew, we would catch the bus to Wolverhampton and visit a shop called 'The Band Box' in Snow Hill, the Mecca of many a local musician, alas now closed down. George Taylor Frame had been a singer in the era of the dance bands of the 1920's and 30's and was the proprietor of the establishment. With his strange spectacles, which made one eye look like a small pea and the other like a car headlamp, he watched us like a hawk as we stood by the far wall 'reading' the sheet music, whilst surreptitiously copying the chords to the latest releases with a pen onto the palms of our hands or even a shirt cuff. If he could catch us we were politely, but firmly, asked to leave. How embarrassed we must have looked. In those days we had respect for older ones and left without backchat. He was right after all!

All over the country the music scene was thriving, and there were always advertisements for musicians to join newly forming outfits.

I used to have the occasional knock in the front room of the family home with a couple of lads from college, Reg Brown and Bob Shorthouse, whom I have sadly lost touch with, but eventually I spread my wings and went for several auditions with local bands that were being put together. Being a bit fat, young, unfashionable and inexperienced - and not a very good guitar player, I was unsuccessful. However I was gaining valuable insight into working with other musicians and getting an idea of what would be the expected stage appearance and manner of presentation.

On a Friday or Saturday night, me and my old apprentice mate 'Spud' (real name Roger Tados, taters, spuds, got it?) would make our way on his Bantam 125cc motor bike, with me on the pillion, to a pub called the Oxley Arms to watch great local bands like Harlem and Soul Package. Hearing these sounds only made me more determined than ever to find a soul band to join.

Sometime later, one bank holiday, in the very early days of my music career and during a break in bookings, Spud decided on a camping trip to the seaside at Skegness. He had just finished making his own motor bike, a Tribsa I think it was called. The idea was that a frame from one brand of bike was mated with an engine of another; in this case a BSA frame and a 500cc Triumph engine. He assured me that all would be well; he had just put an MOT on the monster.

We packed a tent and a few spare clothes and we set off in the early morning during a heavy downpour of rain. After a few hours of travelling the sun appeared. Leaning back on the pillion I remember looking out across a vast airfield somewhere near Newark. There were several Vulcan Bombers painted white, lined up on the runway, a very impressive sight. Suddenly, and without warning, the back tyre blew and the inner tube wrapped around the chain sprocket and stopped the wheel dead in its tracks. The road began to move in slow motion up toward me. 'Oh bugger,' I thought, my days of playing were over before they had even started, my life flashed before me. Anyway, we skidded quite a distance; thankfully no other traffic was on the road at the time.

Luckily, the only injuries we sustained were a few bruises and smashed teeth, and my hair was missing from my forehead and the top of my head - crash hats were not compulsory then. We both had a very narrow escape.

My hair never really grew back properly; still we lived to tell the tale. On some of the old poster photographs, I can see the damage done to my scalp; I confess to never having been on a motor bike since!

Scene Two

Little drummer boy

The journey into music proper really began when I was reading the local Wolverhampton Express and Star newspaper one midweek evening. There was an advertisement which appealed to me, it read: 'Wanted, musicians to form Soul band,' and for an interview please call at a house not far from the town centre.

On a cold misty early evening, I caught the bus into town and after a short walk from the bus stop, found the house. It was in a block of 1930's properties not far from a nearby factory which had made parts for Spitfires during the Second World War.

The person who had placed the advertisement was not at home. The front door was opened by his 12 year old daughter Molvia, who was babysitting the other three children, Paul, Andrew and Mark. She explained that her father was working night shifts as a track maintenance man on the railway, and her mother was out, employed by a firm cleaning offices. She said that it would be best to call again and that I had been the first to contact him, and she was sure that her father would be interested in talking to me.

Working class people had to try all ways to make ends meet and provide something better for their children. But even when working so hard, ordinary people never really had much, don't forget that food rationing didn't finish until 1954, and then it took years for the economy to gather momentum before times improved.

Many years later, I learned that Molvia had become an author herself, with a book entitled, 'Perfectly Flawed' by Molvia Maddox, about living with a genetic disease which her own daughter now has to deal with.

With a feeling of excitement and trepidation I returned to the house that weekend for a Saturday afternoon audition, this time taking my guitar. I felt a right twit taking my guitar on the bus, everyone seemed to stare, but not many people had cars in those days and the trolley bus was, for most, the only means of getting around. As I recall there was only one car owner in the street where I lived.

Things have changed a bit since then! Everybody has a car now, and even as many as four or five can be seen on the drives of some houses; and drives, nobody had a drive, you parked the car in the street. At night a little red light had to be attached to the car battery and clipped to the window to warn other motorists that the car was there. I don't know who, there was nobody about after dark, but if the police caught you not displaying your little red light, you were nicked! I find it amazing that over the years various governments have found many ingenious ways of making nearly everybody a criminal! Anyway, the person who was forming the band was a young West Indian man recently over from Manchester, Jamaica who was a part time working drummer, possessing a sparkling new red Premier drum kit, his name was Steryl Williams.

Steryl wanted a band made up of white and black lads rather like the Equals, a successful chart topping band at the time. Due to working a night shift Steryl often didn't greet the day until after two in the afternoon. When he introduced himself, I saw a slim, nice looking young man, older than I was. I noticed the home had a happy feel about it, and too, how the children were respectful, good mannered and well behaved - a far cry from some of the characters that I had already met on my journey so far. He was married to Molly, an English girl and visiting at the same time was Molly's mother, so I was introduced to all the family at once!

We spoke at length, and let the titles of songs ring in the air. Steryl rapped out the rhythms of the tunes with his drumsticks on the arm of a chair and I plonked out the chords as best I could. We hit it off immediately, and by now my interest had been captured. The buzz that one feels when working with other musicians that are on the same wavelength, is inexplicable, a wonderfully visceral experience. He had been around the local West Indian music scene for a while and knew quite a few good singers and guitarists, but he wanted something different from the usual run of the mill pub group. He had the idea to mix soul music with a music I had never heard of, reggae and blue beat or ska, and as I said at the time, 'What was that?!' It wasn't until later that this type of music hit the British charts, and many acts and bands went on to achieve greatness in the field of reggae. He played me several records which he had brought from home (Jamaica), and with me playing along with the chords we decided that this could be 'a goer.' His idea was something different, and I wanted to be part of it. He re-named me 'Bill' after William Shakespeare, a name that in West Indian circles has stuck with me. Even now Steryl's wife and children find it strange to call me Pete, it's always Bill. We agreed to form a band, shook hands and toasted our new friendship with a shot of white rum.

I had kept in touch with Steryl and his family over the years, until recently, when a massive difference of opinion developed between some members of his family and myself concerning religion, they being Jehovah's Witnesses and me now not, more of that nonsense later! Suffice to say that all the years of trust, respect and love have been destroyed by a mind controlling fundamentalist religious cult, and yes, they do divide people and families!

Just up the road from the Oxley Arms was a garage which, on a Saturday night, would throb to the strains of ska and blue beat music. Although we had heard the dull bass and drum beat and saxophone melodies of the music many times as we passed by, we had never been interested in finding out what went on behind the doors - until now! When the singer of the band 'Harlem,' who had been performing at the Oxley Arms that evening, suggested that Spud and me go down to join him at the garage, we readily agreed.

When the pubs closed in those days there were few places to go on to afterward, well, not without costing money, so the garage had become a haunt for night owls who wanted to carry on dancing, or just shoot the breeze with their friends.

The sound proofed garage was situated at the side of a semi-detached property which was surrounded by small factories and was a short distance from the railway sidings and freight yard. The beat of the bass could be felt throbbing in the air as you approached, even above the trains shunting in the railway company's yard. On entering the wicket door one had to make a small contribution, usually about fifty pence, which bought a can of lager or a bottle of barley wine. Barley wine, I found out later, was the drink favoured by musicians because of its high alcohol content and lack of volume. You could get quite relaxed without the feeling of wanting the loo, ideal for those who couldn't just leave the stage when they felt the call of nature. Me and Spud stood there propping up the wall, the only two white blokes in the place. Our awkwardness was short lived as various ones came over and shook our hands. The people inside were really pleased that we had ventured in to make friends with them, and truth to tell we enjoyed ourselves until the early hours, what great music! And I was gathering ideas for tunes that we could play in our new band when it was formed.

Spud liked John Mayall and Peter Green type blues and attempted to play a blues mouth organ. He didn't really care for the type of music I was beginning to listen to, so we ultimately drifted apart as mates. We had some good memories though, even if he did nearly kill me once! Spud and his mother were nice people, but as I said before, music was calling me.

At the time Steryl, or 'Willy' as I now called him (after his surname Williams), was finishing the last bookings with a West Indian band called appropriately 'The Tropicals.' The musicians were almost past retirement age but they had an obvious love of their music and were very kind, hospitable people; I can still remember Sonny on saxophone and George on banjo. The band used to rehearse at one of the band member's houses in Blackacre Road, Dudley. I recall the first time I walked into that front room and the smell of paraffin entered my nostrils! Paraffin heaters were common amongst West Indian families. They initially found England a very cold and damp place;

entirely different to how England had been marketed in Jamaica and on the other Islands, and it came as a bit of a shock to their systems, especially if they arrived here in winter! Most only had a wardrobe of clothes suited to the temperate climate of the West Indies. George and Sonny wore lightweight suits and sported Panama hats. The suit trouser legs were cut wide at the knee and narrowed at the ankle and had turn ups. The younger West Indian chaps called the older men who wore this type of suit the 'baggyfoot' men, I found this so amusing.

The Conservative government of the time had invited commonwealth countries to send people to England to help re-build the country after the war. The first West Indian people to come to 'The Mother Country,' left home for the shores of England on a liner called the 'Windrush' in 1948. Later many more arrived at Heathrow airport in great family groups, all dressed in their Sunday best. By the 1960's and 1970's they became firmly established in the community hoping to become part of an accepted way of life. Many thought that this would be a temporary move and were not intending to stay forever. Sadly though, within a short period of time of arriving in England, some began to experience a lot of colour prejudice. It became hard for the newcomers to find accommodation, nobody wanted them, and an irrational fear began to spread throughout working class areas that they had come to steal their jobs. Sure the culture was different, and they ate different foods, but most only wanted to make a better life for themselves and their families.

At that time, jobs were there for everyone; the country's economy was starting to boom and most of the occupations which the newcomers accepted were ones that a lot of English people didn't want anyway. It happened the same way when the Ugandan Government cleared out Asian families and forced them into moving to other countries. Asian businessmen began to take over the local corner shops. There was a great hue and cry, but remember that before this time, you could not buy a loaf of bread after 7.30 in the evening or a bottle of milk on Sunday, most corner shops were closed! If you ran out of essential supplies, you did without until Monday morning when the shops opened in the village, or you caught the bus to shop in the town or at the market. Now we take it for granted that we can buy our groceries anytime we like, and guess where most of us shop when we get stuck for a loaf or a bottle of wine!

At that time, it appeared that few wanted the jobs on the buses. Perhaps the money could have been better and the hours were too long compared to the conditions and good money that could be earned by a skilled man or an assembly worker on 'piece work' in a factory. Younger ladies wanted to become air hostesses, not nurses anymore.

I remember how the office girls would not be seen dead talking to a craft apprentice if he had oily hands or was dressed in his work overall, and most fancied themselves as 'glamour pussies.' Everybody wanted something better than the manual labour their parents had done before the war. If you were a young man who worked in an office and drove a sports car you were in, so it appeared that as people became more affluent, prejudice of all descriptions began to rear its ugly head.

Today it's sad to learn that many older ones, returning back to the Caribbean, experience prejudice of another kind. Many saved up enough money to return to the West Indies after a lifetime of living and working in England, and were looking forward to retiring back home. However, when they made it back, they were called 'foreigners' by people with whom they had grown up, gone to school with and who had lived in the same village or town, aren't human beings silly!

Selfishness and hate has never improved the lot of any of the human race. I found this hatred to be very wrong, as all the West Indian people I had met were in England to work.

Many of Willy's friends worked on the railway. These men worked nights repairing the tracks using their brute force and strength in all weathers and seasons, to provide a future for their kids. Good, honest, hardworking men; men like Isaac, George Codner, and Keith (Blackeye), who ran his own lorry business. A lot of the young ladies who followed the band were nurses and worked long shifts. All of them accepted me as I was, and were exceedingly kind to me (although I was always very shy when it came to the ladies and they used to tease me rotten).

The biggest amount of prejudice that I came across was from other white lads who didn't like the fact that I was friends with West Indians, and in some clubs the black lads didn't like me in 'their' club either - and all I wanted to do was play music! There have been several occasions when drunken blokes, white and black, wanted to beat me up because of my associations; anyway, that silliness is all best forgotten. I am glad that this generation is a little more understanding and tolerant, well, I hope they are.

Willy invited me to a couple of rehearsals with the Tropicals and suggested that I join the band on stage for just one night. The other band members didn't seem to mind and as it was his last booking with them, Willy felt that I would gain some stage experience. I certainly gained something! My job was to inject a bit of rhythm and lead guitar. Oh my, that was many years ago now but I will never forget it.

The booking was at the Winson Green Community Centre, Birmingham, and on a warm Bank Holiday evening we took to the stage, how do I remember? I remember because it was a baptism of fire! Within moments of the opening chords and words of, 'Oh when de saints go marchin' in,' performed in a blue beat style, a hail of half eaten food, rice and chips and bottles hit the stage! Followed closely by several well aimed chairs! Panic ensued, fighting broke out everywhere. We had long left the venue before the 1am close down. That night, on the way home from the disaster, I had to ask Willy what several new swearwords meant! The audience were not best pleased; Willy just sat there, grinning. Now I knew why he wanted to form his own band!

During this sojourn I came across one of their business cards. I have kept a few odd bits and pieces. I am glad that I did.

These old stagers are probably gone now, but they played their part in entertaining other West Indian people around the Birmingham and Dudley area, helping them feel more at home in a new land. George and Sonny were happy and friendly men, but the music had moved on and unfortunately they were left a bit behind. The strange thing is that George had a son named Naftel who was a great singer. He could have been a big star but chose not to enter the business. I don't think that the Tropicals played again after Winson Green, I guess they hung up their instruments and bowed to the inevitable. Reggae, with its more edgy rhythm, was slowly replacing blue beat and was, for the younger people, easier to dance to. Some of the dancing could be seen as quite provocative, especially when the young lady moved her body to the rhythm of the music over your knee, and you did the same with her! I couldn't do that now, I would put my back out!

Here is the poster advertising that fateful event.

THE PROGRESSIVE THRIFT CLUB

proudly presents

EASTER MONDAY
DAY & NIGHT DANCE

at the

Winson Green Community Centre
212 Winson Green Road

———x———

MUSIC BY THE SUCCESSFUL
Tropicals Soul and Jazz Group
(from DUDLEY) and
Alton's Heart Breaker Sound System

———x———

Admission 8/-   4.30 – 1 a.m.

Curried Rice and Patties

———x———

'Buses 11 and 96 to door; 82 to 87 to Winson Green Road

Printed by E. H. Russell and Co. Ltd., 1 Park Lane, Birmingham, 6.   359 2723.

Several weeks earlier, Steryl had asked another musician to join his new band. He had worked with Roger Osbourne in the past in a little outfit called 'The Blue Birds.' Steryl and Roger enjoyed reminiscing about their time at 'camp,' the summer camps in the West Indies arranged by local schools, giving the opportunity for young people to meet others and develop social skills; they had a lot in common and got on well.

Roger was a very respectful man, with impeccable manners. He was married to an English girl, Elizabeth, and together they had several children. He had a ready smile and a good sense of humour. He played rhythm guitar and used a red Hofner the same as I did, so immediately we established a good rapport. His love of music was quite broad and often he enjoyed playing and singing Nat King Cole type songs, eventually singing a couple of numbers in the new band when the vocalist went backstage to change into another costume. He could be a crafty one though. He would slowly turn down the volume of his amplifier during the show. When the sound didn't feel right and we found him out, he said he wanted to make the speakers last longer! After a few sharp words we only laughed. He did a great version of 'Walking The Dog,' by Rufus Thomas and exuded happiness when he sang.

We spent many happy times together along with his brother Cal, especially when waiting to go on stage. Sometimes at a club we used to watch the older men playing dominoes in a back room. It was so funny when they played fives and threes. When it came to their own turn to play they would put down the domino by starting, arm up and fully outstretched, and then send it smashing on to the table, at the same time giving an almighty shout. The drinks would shoot up off the table and everyone would laugh, happy days. Sometimes it might get a bit heated if someone put down a silly domino or knocked the table, indicating that they could not add to the chain at a crucial moment, but for the most part the games we watched were friendly affairs. I liked Roger, sadly I heard that he had died several years ago. He was a good man and will be sadly missed by all who knew him.

In the new, as yet unnamed band, I was to be on lead guitar, Roger on rhythm guitar and Willy on drums and another old friend of Willy's, Lloyd Letman from Barbados was to be on saxophone, but we still needed a bass player and someone who could sing.

Things were slow moving to start with, and I remember Steryl and I had little money one Christmas, to be fair, we were skint. On a foggy night, we came out of the Y.M.C.A. where Steryl had been arranging a rehearsal room and popped next door to a public house called the Limerick. We had half a bitter each then turned out our pockets, between us we rustled up enough to buy a half bottle of rum. On returning to Willy's house to share our miseries we hoped that the New Year would bring us a change in fortunes.

One Saturday morning, the following spring, whilst browsing in a music shop in Dudley in the West Midlands, Willy found himself talking to a bass player who had a friend who wanted to be a singer. Finally, we now had our band.

I wondered whether we would ever be able to break out, things were taking an age to get going. We certainly all had ambition, were willing to sacrifice our time in rehearsing, and were prepared to spend time away from home and family in the search to make something of ourselves. We loved our music and appeared to all want the same thing. Looking at the first band photograph now, I appear to have been startled by the photo flash! I was nearly seventeen with a pocketful of ambition and instead of day dreaming, like most of the boys who played a guitar that I went to school with, I was about to step out into the big world. Where would it lead?

As an apprentice in those days of the 1960's and early 70's, the code of dress was a collar and tie for work. Our hair was always neatly cut, usually in a square neck style, and in most respects we resembled a mini version of an 'older' adult. As I began to 'feel my feet' as it were, I dared to cast off the monthly haircut and developed a sort of Jimi Hendrix frizz. This did not go down well both at home or in the factory, and there were those who started to think that I had become rebellious and therefore I should be 'watched' carefully. I always found support from an old stager called 'Tiger' Tom Blower, now a labourer at the factory (more of Tom later). He used to regale me with show business tales of when he played in the big band era, only fuelling my desire to break out. Occasionally, I received telephone calls re-directed from the works office to the tool room for me, prompting much talk and whispering that, 'It's becoming his office, the cheeky little bugger.'

The goings on in my life became the talk of the factory and even some old school pals became jealous and had begun to call me Mr Popstar man, even though I didn't play pop music and had not yet gigged properly with the new band. I am glad that I didn't give in to peer pressure and stop playing my guitar (it would have been easy to do, feeling a little embarrassed at the attention), but this was something I had to get used to. If I had given in, I would not have had the great adventure that I am now able to talk about.

Most of the people who I grew up with are still sat on the same bar stool in the same pub, mostly divorced, having never progressed much farther than the factory, what a waste!

This life is not a dress rehearsal, so my advice, such as it is, is to live it to the fullest manner that you can, but keep it honest and clean and be true to yourself. If you listen to too many people you may wake up one morning wondering where all the years have gone and wishing that you had done more with your life. Most people are basically cowards and hate anyone who doesn't run with the pack, if you run with the pack you can be controlled. Having boundaries and guidelines for our behaviour is good and beneficial if the controlling factor will make you a better person, more honest, loving and kind, but usually you become the slave of other people's ideals and ideas, 'stick in the mud's' who for the most part have mucked up their own life and want to control yours. So go for it!

Even now I have so much more I want to do and achieve. I feel that it is wrong to live life through other people, go out and have a go, do something positive with your life, you never know, you just might become successful.

'Remember that the person going nowhere usually gets there.'

So how do you judge success? A few years later when I gave in and realised that my music career had stalled, I took a management position within a large company. I had a line manager who was showing off in front of the sales staff pontificating that he was a successful man because he had been promoted and his new shiny company car was waiting for him on the works car park. Ever the big mouth, I enquired, 'By whose standards are you a success?'

You do not judge a person's success in life by how much he earns, how big his car or ego is, surely not. Isn't it really a lot of little things? How well have the kids turned out, have they become responsible human beings? Maybe you have stuck by someone through thick and thin, or followed a dream and played the game. Can you look the world in the eye and honestly say that you gave of your best?

I consider that men like Steryl, Roger and Cal were successful men, along with many others who I worked with in show business; although none of us made the really big time, we tried our hardest and for the most part enjoyed ourselves. I cannot put the description of a successful person better than Theodore Roosevelt who wrote:-

'It's not the critic who counts, not the one who points out how the strong man stumbled, or how the doer of deeds might have done them better.

The credit belongs to the man who is actually in the arena; whose face is marred with sweat dust and blood, who strives valiantly; who errs and comes up short again and again; who knows the great enthusiasms, the great devotions and spends himself in a worthy cause and who, at best, knows the triumph of high achievement, and who at worst, if he fails at least fails while daring greatly, so that his place shall never be with those cold and timid souls who know neither victory or defeat.'

(Theodore Roosevelt, 1858-1919, 26th US President and 1906 Nobel Peace Prize Winner).

Dressing nicely was a passion for all of the lads; we always tried to put up a good impression wherever we went. I had observed that most of the guys in the audience dressed really smartly; an outing to a club was something to dress up for, and the ladies too always made a special effort to look nice. I see young ladies going into night clubs today so scantily dressed that they appear to be liable to catching a cold! Long evening gowns used to be the order of the day for the ladies, adorned with their favourite jewellery. Most had their hair in curlers from about lunchtime in preparation for a big night out. The accepted dress code for the men was a nice suit and the biggest silk hanky left flowing from the top pocket of the suit jacket. With a lace shirt and a nice tie we all looked a bit like peacocks; a style that I liked and copied.

I used to paint my shoes all colours - green, blue or red - you could buy leather paint from a cobbler in Wolverhampton. I once met a couple who saw Joe Cocker in a fish and chip shop late one night in Crookes, Sheffield, and all they could comment on, in disgust, was the fact that he had silver shoes with stars painted on them, it may have looked unusual to other people, but that is what we did! That's show business.

Some, like Keith the lorry owner, wore dark glasses in an attempt to look cool, earning himself the title 'Blackeye.'

It wouldn't do for me to wear dark glasses, I can hardly see as it is. My old foreman, Jack, always told me I would go blind - I don't know what he meant! However, I did once consider wearing dark specs to help stop the glare of the stage lights, but it felt as if I was doing the 'star' bit - although I would wear them for publicity photographs.

I don't know why we decided to settle on the name 'The Reason Why.' Looking back it was not a very good name, but it did capture peoples' imagination, so I guess it must have worked. We all have a degree in hindsight don't we?

A young lady named Josie, a friend of Willy's wife, painted

the band's new name on a piece of leather cloth which fitted to the bass drum. The artwork, drawn predominantly in red, fitted in well, as we were attempting to put together a red theme for the stage show. Roger and I both had red guitars, Willy had red glittery drums and eventually, we all wore red crushed velvet trousers with sparkly silver tops, except for Jimmy vocals who wore a red cape with a red shirt and black trousers.

This, for the most part, was how we kept our stage appearance and we always tried to maintain the equipment so that everything gave the impression of a professional show.

On stage, all the chrome of Willy's drums glistened and the guitars were polished so that no sweaty finger marks could be seen! With this type of show, it is attention to detail that makes the difference. (I have seen bands with speaker cloths ripped and filthy equipment, and although the musicians could be very competent, invariably it gave the impression that they were only playing at what they did.)

Although one gets tired on tour, attending to the appearance of the gear can be therapeutic and can prepare the mind for the evening's performance

.

Scene Three

I'm a soul man!

Rehearsals with the new band began in the Y.M.C.A. cellars in Wolverhampton, a place where Willy had rehearsed previously with other budding stars.

Finding rehearsal rooms was difficult because of the volume of sound produced by the bands, people living in close proximity to the public house didn't want the noise, and because there were so many new outfits being formed, suitable rooms came at a premium price. But as always, ever the ones to make a quick buck, some pub landlords would have a band in each of their spare rooms; you can imagine the cacophony of noise.

The cellar was approached down a set of stone stairs descending deep into the bowels of the Y.M.C.A. building in Westbury Street, now a Sikh Temple. It smelled of damp, but due to the thickness of the walls, we could make as much noise as we liked without disturbing the neighbours in the Limerick pub next door. Rather than take all the equipment down and pack it away after each session, we were given a key to the cellar and could leave the gear set up. We would arrive by bus, let ourselves in and then make our way underground - like moles disappearing from the light of day.

We practised three to four nights each week; the sessions getting longer as our repertoire increased. After rehearsals I usually managed to catch the last bus home at eleven o'clock leaving from the town centre.

As the public houses called, 'Time gentlemen!' and spilled their flotsam and jetsam into the streets, there was always the local alcoholic that you tried to avoid. Hoping that he would not sit next to you on the bus, one made an effort to find a seat on the upper deck as far away from the stairs as possible, often to no avail as the last journey of the evening was always pretty crowded. It was a regular routine, the same nutter, and the same bus stop outside the same pub. As the bus stopped outside a long gone establishment called 'The Bulls Head' the same silly chap staggered on to the bus to alight his magic carpet and wobble his way up the stairs.

He was a short, thin man, and had the worn appearance of an old building labourer with cement caked hobnail boots and a ruddy complexion showing the many years spent outdoors in all weathers. He wore a battered flat cap and had a half smoked cigarette stub behind his ear. He had brown, nicotine stained fingers and bloodshot eyes peering through bottle end glasses. A sad soul really.

You knew that if you found yourself a vacant seat near the stairs and the other half was free, he would make a bee line for it and drop himself down heavily next to you. You would then avoid conversation by fixing your gaze out of the window and thus steer clear of eye contact - there was no escaping until the terminus.

The poor man always gave the impression that he was about to vomit by belching and appearing to regurgitate the contents of his stomach, and the fumes were enough to fill the bus. After a few minutes of belching and farting, the fool would begin to sing something like, 'Show me the way to go home' whilst stamping his hobnail boot on the metal floor of the upper deck to beat out the rhythm. This would start a chorus of abuse from the jolly younger men, usually seated at the rear of the bus,

'Shut up,' 'What a racket,' 'You can't sing,' ......and other expressions that are unprintable, could be heard above the peals of taunting laughter, whereupon the drunk would stop the singing. He would turn around and glare through his bottle end glasses at the seated passengers, then wobble to his feet. After a bit more belching and loud farting he would shout,

'Who said that?' then sit down heavily and begin singing again.

The process was repeated several times until getting into a rage he would thrust his leg into the aisle and begin to wag it about in a kicking motion and shout,

'Who said that? I'll put one of these in your face!' pointing to his hobnail boot.

By this time the crowd would begin to drive the fool mad; his now red face would begin to turn blue with anger and all through the journey he would be constantly threatening to 'Put one of these in your face.' Many passengers would be crying with laughter at the nightly entertainment on the upper deck. I suppose today he would be found beaten to death and robbed in an alley, but back then he was seen as a harmless fool and left to live life as he wanted.

Occasionally some of the boys and girls who used the facilities of the youth club at the Y.M.C.A. would come into the cellar to watch us rehearse. We met some really nice young folks there. I liked the fact that prejudice did not appear to be an issue.

After we had been rehearsing for a few months, as well as getting the musical arrangements and running programme right, we began to look for ideas for stage wear. Presenting the right professional image would show that we meant business. A lot of the English bands wore denim jeans and tee shirts, which was all well and good if you were a 'progressive rock' outfit, but we were not. We felt that we needed to seek inspiration from the Motown stable. They always appeared smartly dressed and were able to put on fabulous shows - the sort we had in mind. The white and black music scene was virtually separate; back then they had their own agencies and most English musicians preferred either the chart pop music of the time, rock and roll, or the newly emerging 'progressive rock,' and rarely did we meet. Even those who had been good drinking buddies thought it strange for me to be interested in the world of reggae. Thankfully it's now accepted as great music.

Now and then, Willy and I used to call in to a nightclub in Wolverhampton owned by Mr Uccellini, who himself had a well known band called 'Giorgio and Marco's Men,' if my memory serves me correctly. At this club we would watch the show of a band called 'The Ebonies' - the best and most well known black band in Wolverhampton at that time. The Ebonies were a four piece band whose stage appearance and performance was immaculate. They wore red crushed velvet trousers and white shoes and looked extremely smart. We liked the idea of the band moving as a unit, including having stage dance steps. Eventually, the Ebonies became a very big act in Denmark, having chart success in that country.

Willy knew a talented dressmaker, Gwen Jones, who was a friend of Willy's wife Molly. She was a smiley, happy person who was very kind to me and I loved her company. She agreed to design and make our outfits. She used Asian Indian type material of various fabrics and colours to fashion a range of shirts for us. When we took to the stage we looked the biz!

We also decided to complement our shirts with red chiffon like scarves and red crushed velvet trousers with a black line along the seam. So, we had the clothes, almost had a show, but no means of transportation to the gigs that we had yet to get!

Occasionally, we frequented a striptease club called 'The Cosmo Club,' on the Dudley Road. I think it was two terraced houses knocked into one. It had more than its fair share of men dressed in crumpled mackintoshes, with one hand in their pocket and having steamed up spectacles, sitting in the shadows watching the girls do their thing, and making a pint of beer last for hours. It's strange that Les Dawson impersonated this sort of person to a tee with his character 'Cosmo' - I wonder if he ever visited the establishment? When we walked into the club and if the dancer knew us, we would get a quick wave and a smile. What some of them could do with a pair of spinning tassels was quite hypnotic. Most of the girls were just ordinary housewives with families to feed, although judging by the size of some of the ladies chests they could feed a crèche! Sometimes they would just pop out of the house to do their act, then go home to the old man (husband).

It may sound silly, but after a while you were used to the ladies performing, and took no notice of them whatsoever. We primarily went there to meet other musicians and get an idea of who was joining who, where they were playing and what the going payment rates were (no, honestly). But I did see one of the musicians having a kiss and cuddle backstage one night with one of the dancers. This drummer had a part in the show which they called his 'stand up routine.' This was where he played a drum solo, standing up, obviously. It proved a little more difficult for him on this particular night, having to play using three sticks! I bumped into him several months later and remarked how he appeared to be having a nice time the last time I saw him, 'Yeah,' he said, 'I was mate; I dropped her in the club!'

There were few 'late night' places in those days; the country's economy was booming and people could not stay out all hours because of having to be at work the next day.

A lot of the major firms also had a nightshift working, and most men were in full time employment, so the clubs were never full in the middle of the week. At weekends it was quite different, when the sign, 'House Full' would be displayed outside as early as 9.30 in the evening.

Jimmy, the vocalist had a friend who played the Vox electric organ and who was also seeking a band. We auditioned Eddie Brown, and although he was not a particularly good musician, the sound of the band became a bit more edgy and funky. He promised that he could get us bookings if we could get to them.

Unfortunately, as in all bands, disagreements about percentages and agency fees arose. It began between Lloyd and

Eddie and sadly, Lloyd decided not to pursue his interest with us anymore. Only the future would prove Lloyd right; we should have listened to him, but we all have a degree in hindsight don't we?

We had to find a van suitable to carry all of us and our equipment. Roger's brother Cal drove a 'Commer' mini-bus for the local New Testament Church of God. He kindly offered us the use of their transport, but only if he was allowed to drive it and only if we chipped in with expenses - a saviour! It must be noted that Cal was one of the kindest people one would ever meet and we had many a smile together. I never heard him say or use a bad word against anyone, he was a true gentleman.

As the band began to get tighter, the youth leader at the Y.M.C.A., Mike Todd, an ex-grenadier guardsman, gave us a few dates to play in front of the people visiting the youth centre. This helped us with some practise and stage experience, although it has to be said, the members of the Derby and Joan club cleared the room within minutes of us striking up!

Our first paid booking was a half set at the 'Caves of Dudley.' We performed the show in front of a predominantly white audience, but I'm glad to say we were really well received, helping me to forget the baptism of fire at Winson Green! As the weeks went by we performed at several clubs and weddings locally, but it became obvious that we could not keep relying on the goodwill of Cal and the New Testament

Church to get us to our bookings. It was also around this time that, to us at least, a very funny situation occurred.

A certain, 'Pastor Brown' -I don't know what denomination he was, but he was certainly West Indian, was caught 'In flagrante delicto' with one of his female parishioners. Apparently, as the story goes, when the unsuspecting husband arrived home early and caught them together, the Pastor, by now white with fear, jumped naked out of the bed and fell to his knees. His last words were, 'Oh Lord let us pray,' just as he felt the size nine of the offended husband's boot crack his walnuts, ah, I suppose it puts a new meaning to the expression 'comforting' the flock!

Eventually, as it was looking as though regular bookings would be forthcoming, it was decided that we ought to have our own van. We all resolved that, as the work came in, we would give an equal share towards the purchase of a shiny, nearly new, blue Transit van. Eddie Brown volunteered to be its keeper and as he was a mechanic for the local bus company, would carry out the routine servicing.

When we were booked for a show, each member of the band had to find their own way to the Y.M.C.A., usually by bus, except Eddie who brought the van from its garage in Dudley to collect us all. Mostly this meant an early afternoon start catching the bus into town carrying a suit case with neatly packed stage outfits. Sometimes, if we had to make a sea crossing for a gig, then a 4am start was required. A Royal Iris booking meant a morning 10 o'clock muster, anyway we were very often still groggy from the night before and feeling knackered before we started, but we had to have enough time to load the equipment and make the engagement.

As our confidence and stage proficiency grew, we began to receive a string of bookings from all over the country, but we had a favourite club in Handsworth Birmingham, situated on the Soho Road, called 'The Santa Rosa.' This club was where we had the pleasure of meeting and working with some of the greatest stars of Reggae. When we were not performing ourselves, we enjoyed watching as many of the acts as possible, but often we appeared on the same bill.

The Independence Day dances and functions were usually something special. We once appeared on a sort of variety show for the Jamaican and Barbadian Ambassadors. One of the female dancers performed with the most enormous python I had ever seen, well to tell the truth I had never seen a python before and we were all a bit nervous of it. Its body was as big as the lady's waist; heaven knows what she fed him on! She kept the snake in the dressing room, albeit in a cage, but unfortunately this only served to upset the rest of the performers on the show and no one would enter the dressing room without the female keeper on hand.

One of the turns ate fire, bit into light bulbs and chewed razor blades! No kidding!! He washed them down with a pint of best bitter. The silliest act that I recall was when working in another club in Birmingham; a young man took off his shirt and asked a lady from the audience to draw two lines on his back using white chalk. From his pocket he then produced a set of darts and invited someone else from the audience to throw the darts into his back, but 'Please,' he asked, 'not inside the white lines because that is where my lungs are!' I've seen some funny things, all in the name of show business.

One singer of a rock group which I worked with for a short time, was being heckled from the audience, they didn't like his catawalling voice! He promptly jumped into the crowd swinging the mike stand around his head, knocking several people out for the count, this caused a riot and fighting broke out everywhere.

I recall a booking with 'Reason Why' at Cowley in Oxfordshire. We had travelled all day in our new van; the weather was hot and we had had nothing to eat. Jimmy the bass player decided to grab some soup from a Chinese restaurant and left us to set up the back line (amplification) without him. It transpired that he had drunk a pint of iced coke along with the Chinese spicy soup and suddenly, realising that we were on stage in a few minutes, ran from the restaurant into the Assembly Hall and up a large flight of stairs. On reaching the top of the stairs, the coke bubbled forth from his stomach and down his nose and the poor lad vomited violently, slipped in the mess and caught every marble step on the way back to where he started. He was carted off to the hospital and I had to learn very quickly how to blag my way through bass guitar.

On the way home, a saddened Jimmy Bass fell asleep exhausted in the van, his mouth open and snoring. Eddie decided to roll up a page of newspaper, insert it into Jimmy's mouth and light the end. He awoke just in time to save his facial hair! Musicians are always doing things like this, winding each other up; it makes for some light entertainment and breaks up the monotony of the travelling.

I remember when I did a short stint with a band who had told the young inexperienced drummer that he had caught the 'crabs.' What had happened was that he fancied a barmaid who worked in the hotel where we were booked to play for the weekend - and he had been caught having a kiss and cuddle with the willing participant.

The older boys poked a bit of fun at him, teasing him about not messing with 'dirty girls' and frightening the poor fool into being convinced that he had indeed gotten a bit too close to the girl and must have caught some loathsome disease, and that his mother must never find out or she would kill him! After our second show, during the early hours, in the darkness of the dormitory room where we were all sleeping, a couple of the lad's sprinkled itching powder in the gullible drummer's bed. When he awoke late the next morning he was seen furtively scratching himself. Upon enquiry from one of the band members as to what was the matter, he said that he was itching. All the band members gathered around the wide eyed innocent and pronounced judgement that he had indeed caught a dose of the 'crabs' off this girl. He sulked for the rest of the weekend!

During the return journey back to the Midlands, the drummer snivelled quietly in the back of the van, the boys still continuing to offer advice about lying in a bath of cold water for several days or painting his privates with paraffin and other fantastic cures in order to rid himself of this abominable curse! As the van drew up outside his house, in quite a well to do area of Wolverhampton, his mother opened the front door to welcome her little boy home.

'All right son?' she asked.

His reply was, 'No mum, I've caught the crabs!'

The silly lad was last heard wailing and seen being

forcefully slapped into the house by his mother. As we drove off I'm sure the neighbours must have heard the peals of laughter coming out of the van from many yards away.

Some bands are just simply dirty. Pre 'Reason Why' I had a couple of rehearsals in the back room of a public house with some lads that didn't like me, and I didn't like them, we just didn't click. It came to a head when the drummer (not another one) whilst in full paradiddle, snapped the bolt holding his shiny stool together and fell backwards, still beating the air as he went. I am afraid I lost it and couldn't hold up for the giggles and was promptly told by the rest of his cronies in the band not to laugh at 'our mate.' With long faces they began to pack up the gear and load their untidy van. In the darkness, taking the gear to the van across the public house lawn, one of them collected some dog mess on his shoe which had been deposited by the landlord's Alsatian. They thought this was a real delight. It turned out that as they hadn't used up the full evening on rehearsing they felt that they were due a rebate on the price of the room. No rebate was forthcoming, so as they left, they took it in turns to spread the godsend all over and into the landlord's function room carpet! I bagged the window seat in the van and kept it open all the way to my dropping off point. I never saw them again!

Another time I recall a musician who decided to cycle to keep fit before embarking on a European tour. Whilst out riding one day he found he was approaching a steep hill and decided to hitch a lift up the hill by grabbing hold of the metal bar at the rear of a slow moving tipper wagon carrying sand. Unfortunately, as he pulled on the bar, the rear of the tipper opened and the silly man found himself buried up to his neck in the contents of the lorry. Passing motorists and a policeman had to dig him out with their bare hands, probably saving his skin!

Another outfit I worked with could not afford to buy diesel for the van, so they used to raid building sites and in the darkness nick the stuff out of large metal barrels reserved for the site machinery. I knew that we couldn't work together; if ever we were found out we would surely land up in prison! When I was asked to participate in the escapade I kept well away, refusing to get involved. The old van they used had rotten floorboards. By the time we got to the gigs we were all hallucinating through breathing in the diesel fumes!! When they came to collect me for a gig one evening, they announced that they had got a new light show. This will be good I thought. When all the stage gear and amplification was set up for the show they went to the van and returned with several of the orange lights that are used to notify road users of a hole in the road, you know, the flashing yellow ones; trouble was, the dimwits didn't know how to turn them off and the silly things flashed until the batteries ran out weeks later!

I realised, quite by accident, that I had the possibility of a good blues singing voice. I was rehearsing with a four piece band in the back of another now demolished public house called 'The Travellers Rest,' where the singer at the time was making a mess of Percy Sledge's 'When A Man Loves A Woman.' I was getting more and more annoyed as we had stopped and started the song umpteen times and my patience and fingers were getting sore. Rudely, I grabbed the mike stand and let out the opening lines of the song. Bless me, where did that come from I thought, in tune, full key, everything! I left them the same evening, realising that messing about wasting time was not my idea of progress.

There was a brief spell when 'The Reason Why' performed as a five piece; Eddie Brown had been admitted into hospital for a stomach ulcer operation. One Saturday evening, on the way to a gig in Birmingham, we visited the hospital dressed in our stage gear to cheer him up and bring a little bit of pleasure to the nurses working there. It was nice of the staff and nurses, dressed in their uniforms and white lab coats, to line the outside balconies of the hospital to wave us off as we left the building.

Occasionally, Lloyd Beck, a young piano player would join us for a couple of numbers using Eddie's Vox organ; he was a really good musician. We would have preferred him in the band but he could not afford his own organ and couldn't get us bookings! I saw him on a B.B.C. programme about families who were seeking to find each other. I met up with him some years later under different circumstances when I found out that he too had become a Jehovah's Witness.

My first experience of sailing on a ferry was when I was about ten years old. A school trip took us to board a boat in Liverpool to travel to Llandudno, it was called the St Tudno. Incidentally, Ringo Starr worked the boat as a lad, in an attempt to gain experience for his merchant seaman's ticket. She was beautifully fitted out with mahogany and polished brass and I delighted in the sounds and smells of the steam engine. (She was scrapped in Belgium at Ghent in 1963.)

Because of this earlier recollection, one of the happiest bookings where we regularly performed was on the 'Royal Iris' ferry boat out of Liverpool. She was known as the 'fish and chip boat,' because they served this delicious treat in the below decks restaurant. (In my spare time I enjoy scratch building model boats as a hobby. I would love to build a model of the old ferry, perhaps if I can obtain some blue prints I will.) Every great act from the 1960's must have performed on her stage, from the Beatles to the Searchers and Gerry and the Pacemakers to Acker Bilk and I was thrilled to be able to stand on the same spot as these great working bands and heroes.

Loading the gear on to the boat was always a palaver as we had to carry everything down the long covered walkways to the landing stage then hump it all up the stairs to the ballroom on 'B' deck. The ballroom was 60 foot by 40 foot and she was licensed to carry 1000 passengers when she was river cruising.

The ferry pitched a little as the mouth of the river was passed and it entered open water, then the swell of the river current and the waves from the sea made the boat roll to the left or right (port or starboard). However, nothing stopped the dancers enjoying themselves, they simply followed the movement, whichever way the boat rolled the dancers followed, it was quite funny to watch, but not so funny if there was a bigger wave. There were many occasions when I nearly lost my balance; it's not easy to play a guitar whilst holding on to something and trying to remain upright at the same time! It got really hot on that small stage, the audiences were right up close and without much effort you could dance with them if you had a mind to. Unfortunately, by this time, the boat was getting on a bit and was in need of a re-fit. Several times during a show the electric fuse board would blow, rendering the amps silent and the lights would then go out plunging everyone into darkness. As the lights came back on again and we struck up the band once more, there would be a big cheer from the audience - happy times. We always carried a box of spare fuses and a torch when we knew that we were booked to play on the 'Royal Iris!'

Between sets, one of my favourite things was to go up on to the top of the boat, 'A' deck, and look at the distant shore lights and flashing beams from the lighthouses in Liverpool bay. After the sweatbox of the ballroom below, it was bloody cold standing there on the windy deck, but because of this one could at least grab a quiet moment to oneself and get a bit of fresh air.

It was amazing how the smells of industry from the shore carried for miles on the wind. Ships lights too, seemed so much brighter at sea, standing out against the inky black night sky. A dull thump, thump, thump of diesel engines and a splashing, swishing sound would be heard from the propellers of large ships approaching the mouth of the river, as they made their way into the port. They would appear out of the darkness, blocking out the shore lights. The port was still quite busy then and craft could be seen plying up and down the river at all hours.

I loved Liverpool and its music. I was discussing the earthy sound and the rise of Liverpool music at a party with an old pal of mine, Dave Hill (Slade), some time ago; incidentally Dave is a fine writer and musician in his own right. We both agreed that by listening to the early work of the Beatles you can almost feel the cold wind off the Mersey. Play something like, 'In My Life,' and see if you get what I mean, but it's probably my imagination. I found the people friendly, and a city with a vibrant atmosphere.

In later times, the city was ravaged by a severe recession due to political policies and changes in the way that freight was shipped across the world. I went back some years later and couldn't believe the amount of decay and how empty the river seemed.

I came across an advertising ticket to promote a cruise down the river Mersey on the 'Royal Iris,' one of the many we took, but this one included a trip to the Illuminations at Blackpool, the year was 1969. My factory days now seemed a long way away.

Along with the passengers, we boarded the coaches outside the Gaumont Cinema, Wolverhampton - again all gone now - but we used to be able to take a capacity crowd with us to be the audience and to dance the night away. It was nice to be among such a happy throng of people and we appreciated their loyal support.

It was around this time that I changed my Selmer amp for a new 100watt Marshall rig. The rep said that I had the first off the production line with red leather cloth covering; I loved it and felt that we were now making progress.

Sadly the 'Royal Iris' was eventually sold off and at the time of writing is languishing at Tilbury near the Thames Barrier. She is beginning to list badly due to a fire on board and looks the worse for wear. Although there is a petition to bring her back to the Mersey, I doubt it will ever happen, but I would encourage everyone to give support to the grand old lady. Wouldn't it be great to see the river dance cruises start up again, the sounds of merriment floating on the wind across the Mersey once more?

There were some really nice clubs around at that time where we enjoyed performing, The Cedar Club, the Ridgeway Georgia and the Santa Rosa in Birmingham, The Shades in Sheffield and the Bamboo in Bristol, although here I found that there was a lot of prejudice in the area of Saint Paul's. I understood that this club was the first in the area to be opened especially to cater for West Indian people, but we were jeered and threatened by some white youth as we unloaded our gear into the club, it was very disconcerting.

By kind permission of: Paul Townsend Bristolpast.

We had the pleasure of working for many West Indian

Organisations, entertaining people of all ages, in clubs such as Venn Street, Huddersfield, but it was also nice to play in our own home town and to see our friends and catch up with what had been happening while we were away. It was at the 67 Club in Pipers Row, Wolverhampton, when someone got into our dressing room whilst we were on stage and went through our personal effects, stealing money and watches, jewellery, etc. The thought of a creep doing that made us all feel very uneasy.

At the Woolpack in Wolverhampton, there was a strange arrangement where the stage was positioned in front of a large plate glass window, the sound used to bounce off everywhere!

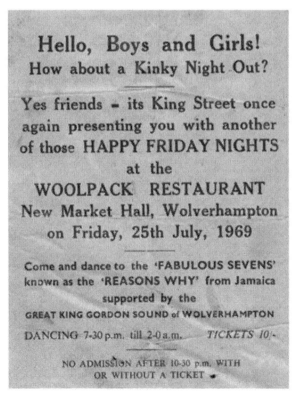

Hello, Boys and Girls!
How about a Kinky Night Out?

Yes friends – its King Street once again presenting you with another of those HAPPY FRIDAY NIGHTS at the
WOOLPACK RESTAURANT
New Market Hall, Wolverhampton
on Friday, 25th July, 1969

Come and dance to the 'FABULOUS SEVENS' known as the 'REASONS WHY' from Jamaica supported by the
GREAT KING GORDON SOUND of WOLVERHAMPTON

DANCING 7-30 p.m. till 2-0 a.m.   *TICKETS 10/-*

NO ADMISSION AFTER 10-30 p.m. WITH OR WITHOUT A TICKET

Authors Collection

There was a real lifesaver for Wolverhampton musicians which I must mention. I have to confess that I would never have remembered the name of 'Snellings' without the help of Billy Howe the author of 'Lost Wolverhampton.' 'Snellings' was the all night chip shop that was located in Snow Hill. Often at weekends, in the early hours of the morning, there would be a row of vans parked outside the shop containing tired and hungry musicians. That may seem strange now, but in those days there were very few places to eat and most dining establishments were closed by about 11 o'clock. After a long journey and feeling tired through the exertions of a show, just to know that you could get a hot meal kept the boys going. The great and the good, the rich and poor, the famous and the unknown could be found dining out, dipping their salty vinegar fingers into a copy of the Express and Star newspaper filled with the most delicious fish and chips, either sitting in the van, or more often than not, huddled in small animated groups on the pavement outside.

I was reading a history of Wolverhampton bands recently and I think only one black band, 'The Ebonies,' was mentioned, sad really because there were several really professional black and mixed race bands around at this time in Wolverhampton. I began to notice early on that there were venues where English bands played that were not available to up and coming black bands. Most of the local 'stars' tended to perform 'pop' type music and work for a small handful of agencies who appeared to be not that keen on having a different type of music on their books, or wanted it performed in front of white audiences at their regular venues. Consequently it was mostly in the black community that black reggae bands became well known. I guess it was Bob Marley who really brought reggae music to the attention of most British youth, particularly when Eric Clapton recorded, 'I Shot the Sheriff.'

It's sad that, although we were all in the same game, there was a lot of snobbery between some of the players, and very often they would like to keep themselves to themselves; a sort of imagined hierarchy I suppose.

However, because we played a different set of venues to the white bands, we never really got to know them - but it's strange that they did know of us. To be fair, they couldn't help it! When we were appearing locally at a particularly large event, Soho Road would be plastered with advertising posters - if you made your way into Birmingham our faces were there for all to see.

Scene Four

A trip to the Isle of Man

When the first migrant workers from the West Indies came to settle in England, in order to help them preserve a feeling of community, they formed local clubs and associations; some were called chalets. Members contributed a small payment each month to a collective fund and this was used to provide events, social evenings and trips, like the one on the advertising poster of a trip to the Isle of Man. This particular outing was arranged for Bank Holiday Monday. I recall that I had just purchased a mohair, handmade, three piece suit, which cost nearly £350 - a lot of money for me, especially in those days. It felt good as we boarded the coach for Liverpool and chatted with the excited passengers, who would become our audience when we performed later that day at the Palace Lido Ballroom in Douglas. There must have been a convoy of at least twenty coaches making their way up the A41 to Liverpool and it looked like we were in for a good evening's show.

We arrived at Liverpool Pier Head to board a boat called the Ben-my-Chree -just as the heavens opened! The boat was fully loaded with parcels, letters and the week's commodities of fruit and vegetables, all destined for the island, and along with our coach parties, space was at a premium. The staff on board had not anticipated the amount of gear we were taking to the Isle of Man and consequently we had to stash most of it on the open deck of the boat. A storm blew up just as we entered the Irish Sea and everything began to roll about the deck; Willy's drums were almost carried over the side by the waves! We had to leave the warmth and comfort of the inner lounge and go up on deck to stand holding the equipment all the way to the island, surrounded by sacks of potatoes, crates of cabbages, carrots and other foodstuffs, all beginning to develop that farmyard aroma! It wasn't a pleasant experience and we were expected to perform later that day.

When we arrived at Douglas harbour, the sun came out, but by now we looked like drowned rats and smelled of wet cabbage, my beautiful new suit was completely wet through. However, as a testimony to the tailor and the material from which the suit was made, when it dried out it looked as though nothing had happened. I think I had that suit for at least another ten years afterward, money well spent! The unfortunate thing was, that as the sun was now shining, the thousand strong audience who had come out on the boat to see the show, decided to spend the day either in the town shopping for souvenirs or making the best of the weather; you couldn't blame them.

We played to an almost empty house, only stalwart fans and family members enjoyed our performance. Someone thought it was a good idea at the time I suppose. Looking at the poster now I like the picture of the old style coach and the price of the venue tickets and note that you could pay for your tickets in instalments! Another little poster, which I came across in my box of treasures, advertises a gig arranged for the West Indian Association Social Club in Venn Street, Huddersfield; it seems many years ago now, but what wonderful stars worked that club.

It is quite rare when other professionals take the time and trouble to complement you on a good performance, and when they do it leaves a lasting impression.

I recall a show at a club in Sheffield called 'The Shades'. Whilst we were round the back loading the van after the performance, a young Englishman and his lady companion made a specific point of approaching me to shake my hand and say how much they had enjoyed it. This man was no other than Joe Cocker and Eileen, his girlfriend at the time. Joe had had a massive hit with the Beatles song, 'With a Little Help from My Friends' during 1968. The story of how Joe got the idea for the song is intriguing. The story told is that Joe was sitting on the lavatory at the bottom of his parent's garden at 38 Tasker Road in Sheffield, when he came up with the idea for the rendition of the song. I suspect that this is an urban myth, but it's a nice story anyway. He rang Chris Stainton with the outline who then added the unforgettable organ introduction and reworked the arrangement into the worldwide hit it was to become.

The show that 'The Reason Why' put on was, by all accounts, pretty awesome and professional. You don't see it yourself when you are part of it. As well as playing on a regular basis, at least three nights a week were dedicated to rehearsals. We also did session work for other performers who hired the band to produce their demo record, one of whom was Ray Martell, who became one of my favourite singers at the time.

You may ask, why practise so much. Well all I can tell you is that practise makes perfect, or as near as you can get to it. After all, if the people coming to see your show are spending their hard earned money, then surely you are honour bound to give them the best you can. I have always found it difficult to work with others who see rehearsal time as time wasted; nothing could be further from the truth. Great Motown and Soul acts rehearsed for hours to get those steps right; watch some of their old video clips and see the pure poetry and grace that these stars had. It didn't come about by accident.

Recently, I was attempting to work with a guitarist who every time we got together, had changed an introduction or chord sequence to a song which we had agreed on and rehearsed many times before. I am afraid that this sort of uncertainty shakes me. I still get nervous enough performing in front of an audience, even after all these years, without having to worry about other musicians. (In all the years that I have watched professionals, like James Taylor perform, they have never altered the format of their great music.)

A performer may have a natural talent, but it has to be honed to be truly professional. Someone may be a great musician, but very often something else is sadly lacking, more often than not it's humility. It makes things difficult and very hard to maintain a long lasting working partnership with this type of person, particularly when egos begin to take over rational thought and the 'indispensable man' begins to dictate affairs. Sadly, it sours relationships, when they realise that there is no such thing! It got to the point where I never knew where I was with this musician and because the cheques were paid into his account he began to develop a nasty habit of holding on to the gig money for as long as he could before shelling out, ooops!! - Been there, done it, never again!! - So I cut the tour short and left it to another act to carry on. I now have a rule that I never work with others unless I have to.

Some musicians I've known decided to turn up for rehearsals if the mood, wife, or girlfriend let them, and they then wondered why they were eventually dropped from the band. Some have turned up just 'in a mood' and refused to play a particular song or riff. When it happens once, one tries to be understanding, but twice means the sack! My advice to any young budding act is that it is not known as Show <u>Business</u> for nothing! Along with your instrument and craft, learn about contracts and the money side of things and develop a hard shell, or you will definitely get ripped off! Don't take any messing about when it comes to money.

Also for what it's worth, be careful committing yourself to another person just as you begin stepping out on your career - most will hold you back. If there are no obstacles placed before you when you start, as the work becomes more demanding, the travelling more frequent and more of your time is taken up with rehearsals, non show business partners will usually start bellyaching and seeking more of your attention. This, in my experience, eventually causes problems down the line, and it's best avoided until your act is firmly established. That's why a lot of show business people marry dancers and such, they know the game, what you are trying to achieve, and understand the sacrifices involved.

Scene Five

It's Show Time

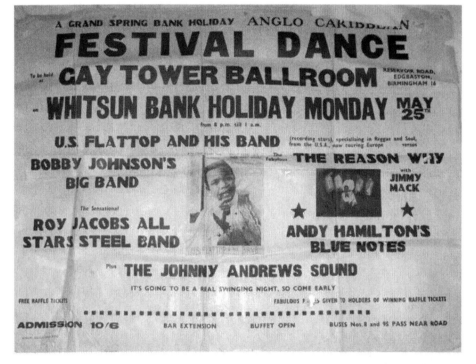

As our reputation began to spread, we travelled all over the U.K. performing shows in night clubs, workingmen's clubs, company dances - wherever anyone would book us. Sometimes, some familiar names from show business would be in the audience; famous acts and musicians, ambassadors and embassy officials, especially at Independence Day celebrations.

We were usually booked to arrive at the venue around 7.30 pm, giving us time to set up the equipment, balance the mikes and do several sound checks. After this there would be a search for somewhere to grab a bite to eat. Fast food is everywhere today, but back then it was a licensed restaurant or fish and chips; Chinese if you were very lucky. On Soho Road in Handsworth, I used to enjoy curry patties with Roger and Cal. I still eat them occasionally when I can find a shop that sells them, but I also loved curried goat, rice and peas and a nutriment drink - go on try some!

A night club show would start at about 11 o'clock with a 'sound.' I recall the massive speaker boxes which the DJ's used, especially made for the job of bringing out the bass notes, and so loud - the thump from the speakers would hit you in the stomach! We would be back stage, dressing and tuning up and Jimmy would run through a couple of songs to warm up his voice. The running order for the show was nearly always the same, a mixture of soul, reggae and ballad tunes, something to shake your hips to and something to attract a pretty girl to dance close to. Then came that stomach churning short silence as the 'sound' ceased and the announcer spoke those fear inspiring words, 'Welcome please, The Reason Why!'

On stepping onto the stage and into the lights you would be temporarily blinded by the glare, but the sound of the crowd made ones hair stand on end, it was electric! There have been quite a few occasions when some in the audience would rush toward the stage to get as close to us as possible, especially if we were performing as support and the headline act hadn't delivered the goods. Sometimes, whilst the main act was on stage, the crowd would chant for 'The Reason Why.'. It was embarrassing, but great for the ego when the 'stars' had to leave the stage early to make way for us. Amongst other venues where I recall this happening was at the Plaza Ballroom in Old Hill near Dudley in the West Midlands.

To start the show Willy would tap, one, two, three, four, by clapping his drum sticks together and we struck up the rhythm and opening bars to 'Freedom Train' by the great James Carr, then to a great roar Jimmy would enter the spotlight. His favourite outfit was a red cape which he would spin round and then fling off into the wings of the stage before beginning to sing; the girls loved him! Throughout the evening we would run through great songs like 'Midnight Hour' by Wilson Picket, 'Ain't too Proud to Beg' by the Temptations ..... in fact, let me put the running order down as we performed it in the show. My memory fails me on some numbers, but from what I do remember, it went something like this; the first and last numbers always being the same:

Freedom Train, James Carr

Midnight Hour, Wilson Picket

Get Ready, The Temptations

These Arms of Mine, Otis Redding

Muriel, Alton and Eddy

Walking the Dog, Rufus Thomas

Montego Bay, Freddie Notes and the Rudies

Monkey Man, The Maytells

Red Red Wine, Tony Tribe

Let your Yeah be Yeah, The Pioneers

Ain't too Proud to Beg, The Temptations

People get Ready, Curtis Mayfield

Israelites, Desmond Dekker and the Aces

Why Birds Follow Spring, Alton Ellis

Bring the Curtain Down, William Bell

When a Man Loves a Woman, Percy Sledge

Bring it On Home to Me, Sam Cooke

Stand by Me, Ben E King

My Girl, Otis Redding

Soul Man, Sam and Dave

Mustang Sally, Wilson Picket

You Don't Know Like I Know, Sam and Dave

Mr Pitiful, Otis Redding

What Am I Living For, Percy Sledge

Knock On Wood, Eddie Floyd

Funky Broadway, Wilson Picket

Goodnight My Love, Jessie Belvin

Cry me a river, Jackie Opel

We were always looking for ideas to 'make show' and I remember once having my hair coloured, one side black, the other side light brown; I must have looked a right pratt, even more so wearing a top hat with a long red ribbon! As I leapt into the air spinning the hat off into the wings, sequins burst out from under it - wow, I wish I could leap today! From the stage we would watch the jigging dancers on the floor; everyone seemed to be having a good time. It was especially nice when the young ladies began to wear red or pink chiffon scarves as a mark that they followed our band and after a while we knew many of the fans by name; but really the girls favourite was Jimmy the singer. He loved doing the 'star' bit and teasing them as to who would be the lucky girl tonight! It was truly a great show and Jimmy could hold an audience spellbound. He used to fall to his knees and pretend to cry when he sang the last ballad. All the girls would try to reach out to touch and comfort the poor sobbing boy - he loved it. But at the end of the show we were all totally exhausted.

Revolving stages always proved to be a nightmare. When you see old footage of the bands coming round on the revolving stage to face the audience at the London Palladium, you may think, 'That looks cool,' but all the ones we worked on were precarious to say the least! The revolving stage in the venue, advertised in the poster from a show at the Tower Ballroom, was a fearsome beast. As the band was performing at the front of the stage, audience side, the follow on act was setting up on the other half, effectively back stage, obviously unseen to the audience. As the applause from the last act faded away, and with the introductions over, it was now your turn to perform. On cue the stage manager gave a pull on a large handle and the platform lurched into life and began to revolve. There have been a few occasions when on coming around to face the audience, we were still trying to maintain balance. One revolving stage almost flung us off because it revolved so fast. We must have looked like the Keystone Cops; we were all holding on for grim death and before we could strike up, had to chase Willy's side drum which was rolling away, and pick up several microphone stands!

We were now gaining experience and the bookings were coming in nicely, and we were establishing a good name for ourselves.

About this time we began recording. We recorded a song called 'Mary Ann' at Chalk Farm studios in London. It was engineered by a man called Phil Chen, who went on to play bass guitar with Rod Stewart's band, and produced by Dandy Livingstone who himself had a hit with 'Bright Lights Big City.' Whatever happened to the record I don't know, I can't find it anywhere.

Sometimes though, we have got it awfully wrong. Whilst performing in a club on the Soho Road in Birmingham one night, during the interval when me and Willy were relaxing - leaning on the wall chatting about the show and drinking a barley wine - a man approached us and said he had written a song. He had been watching the band for a while and asked if we would be interested in playing and recording it, with him singing. Without prompting and in the middle of the nightclub he began to sing a few lines a cappella, but when he reached the part in the song that went:

'As I travel along the White Cliffs of Dover,' we told him to 'go away,' more likely using a more well known expression than that, which means the same. I still think that line is naff, but he had the last word; the man was Jimmy Cliff, the song, 'Many Rivers to Cross.' I can pick 'em can't I? The song is now truly a classic. Well done Jimmy!

One of the worst things about night clubs was the violence. Roger, Cal and me were having a barley wine in a public house a few doors away from a club where we were about to appear, when a man crawled into the bar with blood running from his eyes and ears. The landlord promptly went to fetch - not the police or an ambulance - but his Alsatian dog, and proceeded to drag the man into the road outside the pub! After the show we enquired about the poor man, and heard that he had died in the gutter. It really upset us.

One time, during a lull in bookings, I was asked to accompany a musician friend of mine on one of his gigs. The band which he played with was also of mixed race, English and West Indian lads performing chart pop music. The job was to entertain a wedding party which was celebrating at a working men's club. I was helping to unload the van for them as the wedding party began to arrive. A happy gaggle took their seats in the club and began to fuss the bride and take snapshots; all very lovely. Sadly, one of the wedding guests, a young lady who was heavily pregnant, suddenly collapsed in the car park. Obviously there was great panic and attempts to revive her, but by the time the ambulance arrived it was too late, she had passed away. I can still picture that scene, oh the poor husband and family, all of these things have an effect on you, even though you press on and try to put them out of your mind. The booking money that night was donated to a collection for her and her family; all the audience were shocked and contributed generously. At times like this you see the best in people, it's just a shame that it takes tragedy to bring it out sometimes.

There was all the usual dramatics when a man was found by his wife to be in a club with another woman - which happened on most nights and in almost all clubs. Sometimes it was as if World War had broken out! Fighting would suddenly erupt, glasses and bottles would be thrown, smashing into a million pieces. It's terrible the damage glass can cause to the human face. It made you shake with fear when several of these battles kicked off at once, and you had to clear the stage as quickly as possible to avoid ending up in hospital yourself. Many are the times, whilst packing the gear into the van after a show, that there would be an argument on the car park. Blood could be sent three feet high by some drunken girl slashing her own wrists with a broken bottle because her man had been caught cheating on her. No, I am of the opinion that booze and drugs are no help to thinking straight.

I remember in one club there was an upstairs bar and restaurant. Some crazy maniac decided to kick off and put a table through the plate glass window which overlooked the dance floor, showering large sheets of glass onto the dancers below. Panic ensued, and as people ran up the stairs and tried to enter the restaurant to sort things out, fear stricken folks trying to leave the restaurant at the top of the stairway, began to push. Bodies of people were falling like rag dolls and the sound of screaming was almost unbearable. The show had to be called off.

Another night, Steryl and I were having a quiet drink whilst watching two men gambling at cards. I don't know what game it was; I've never been interested in gambling, and the next few moments would guarantee that I never would be! The interior decor of the club was made to resemble bamboo and palm leaved huts; it had little stalls where one could have a drink and a meal or take to a gaming table and try your luck. As the chips and money began to mount up on the table, people started to be drawn in and gather round to observe the game, their curiosity piqued and the little alcove became crowded. We quietly made our way to the back of the crowd, so that when we had finished our drink, we intended to go back stage and prepare for the show. The crowd became subdued. One of the gentlemen was losing heavily, to the point where his car keys had been thrown into the centre of the table. He was sweating profusely, and then all became silent. In the hushed room, another turn of the cards, another losing hand. The crowd gasped! Finally, his house keys were thrown in to the game. A final turn of the cards and he had lost literally everything. Stunned silence descended on the crowd. Suddenly, the table was hurled into the air, sending the chips, money, keys and drinks everywhere. A World War II bayonet, which had been wrapped in a rolled up newspaper, was produced from nowhere by the loser and was thrust into the stomach of the opponent who had taken all. We shot out of that place quicker than a rabbit with a fox after him, it was frightening and horrible. Even now, if I see someone looking furtive carrying a rolled up newspaper, I think about that incident.

Thankfully, there were funny moments. At an ironing board manufacturing company's annual dinner and dance the managing director got a bit excited. He had been on the whisky a bit too long and began to dance with some of the girls off the assembly line; the sort of dancing movements brought on by a typical older man thinking that he was John Travolta! The girls giggled and slowly began to avoid him, whereupon he fell to his knees and began to beat out the rhythm of the songs on the wooden floor using a 12inch rule. A couple of the directors quietly escorted him away, amidst much furtive whispering behind hands. I wonder how he faced the workforce on Monday morning?

One particular club on the Soho Road, the 'Ridgeway Georgia' had a raised dancing area. Access to the dance floor was gained by about three steps. There was lighting around it arranged in boxes, angled at about forty five degrees, with differently coloured Perspex covers designed to shine up at the dancers; this must have raised the perimeter edge up nearly a metre. The stage for the band was raised up a step or two even higher. On the carpeted floor, around the dancing area, were tables where again one could have a meal and watch the show. Late one evening, a lonely, shabbily dressed lady came into the club. Obviously the worse for wear, she began to dance on her own to the sounds of our band. As the musical rhythms pounded out, she was dancing ever more vigorously, until she ended up dancing too close to the edge of the dance floor. She lost her balance and fell over the angled edge of the lamps and found herself falling head first! She became trapped and entangled in the legs of a dining table and the patrons seated around it! As she desperately tried to extricate herself, several young men gallantly ran over to her rescue. Oh my, it wasn't more than a couple of seconds before one of them shouted, 'The girl has no knickers on!' All the males flooded over to get a peek; most of the audience were by now in fits of laughter, and so were we! - Poor girl!

Another funny moment was when we were at the 'Santa Rosa.' Two Irish lads had had a couple too many and were getting rowdy with each other and shaping up to kick off. It was funny because neither of them could surely see straight. Isaac, one of Willy's workmates from the railway gang, was a giant of a man, strong as an ox yet as gentle as a lamb; he was never seen without a big friendly smile and he was always a peace keeper. He promptly walked over to the lads, raised them off the ground and proceeded to carry them out, one over each shoulder, and deposited them outside the club. The shock shut them both up and I suspect sobered them up pretty quickly!

Thankfully, not all gigs were like a scene from M.A.S.H., but I started to notice the strain getting to me. I began to drink more than I should to try and help me to relax, then I would drink a bit more to help me to sleep, a very silly pattern and habit to develop.

This got me into an embarrassing predicament one New Year's Eve. Just before midnight we were asked by the management of the nightclub if they could use our P.A. system to relay the bells of Big Ben as it struck in the New Year. I decided to find a quiet corner and hide, just me and my bottle. As I entered a little alcove, thinking I was alone, I quaffed a large shot of rum. A predatory lonely female grabbed hold of me, I attempted to fend her off using slurred charm. The alcove was dimly lit, my eyes were swimmy, and all I wanted to do was sleep. As Big Ben struck, so did the girl! She suddenly said, 'Give us a kiss luv,' forcefully grabbed hold of me, and promptly thrust her tongue down my throat! Well, this had never happened to me before; I am afraid that I began to heave and vomited violently all over her!! I have never wanted to die so much before or since. I learned a salutary lesson that night, take Caesar's words to heart, 'Keep your sword by your side and drink alone.' I must confess that I never touch spirits at all now; although I am partial to a bottle of Cabernet Sauvignon with a steak, or a pint of Cobra with my curry.

Another New Years Eve booking was a return to where it all started, Winson Green in Birmingham. This time we were to perform at the Prison Officers Club. The show was to be two sets, one before midnight, the other going on into the early hours. It started well enough, the 'screws' and their wives eating, drinking and dancing away quite happily. As midnight approached and the bells rang out, we waited for the signal to go back on stage for the second half. A couple of the warder's wives, a little the worse for wear, began to argue over someone's husband. Within seconds they started to pull each other's hair out. This led to an almighty fracas and the whole of the audience seemed to take sides - suddenly what appeared to be war broke out! They virtually destroyed the canteen and club room, upturning the tables and sending food and crockery shooting everywhere. Bottles, hair, teeth and fists flew in all directions. We simply peered out from the safety of the dressing room and wondered if we should call the police, oh, we forgot, they were the police! A bloodied officer approached us, paid us up and asked us to leave by a back door as fast as we could; we did not need asking a second time.

The Paradise Lost club in the poster had a bit of a reputation for sexy naughtiness, but if you were seeking a bit of adventure, then most night clubs would find it for you.

One nightclub we worked at was run by a Dutchman. It had several double beds in the upper storey where you could take your pleasure in any way, and with anyone, you chose. I nearly dropped a massive clanger one night at this same club in Birmingham. There was a really attractive young lady serving behind the bar. I remarked on this to Roger and Cal. They began grinning, 'Don't go there Bill!' 'Why not?' I said. They began to giggle even more, 'No Bill, just wait and see,' - a naive lad or what! Because these men were older and had been around the block a bit, they saw something that I didn't. As the club was closing and we were clearing the stage, this lovely 'young lady' began to call for the glasses to be returned to the bar. Oops! This was, you've guessed it, a bloke in drag, and I turned to Roger and Cal only to find them with tears of laughter streaming down their cheeks. I was certainly fooled.

Digs can be odd places too. Somewhere in the North of England we once stayed in what was I think a small hostel, owned by Eastern European people, I certainly didn't recognise the accent. The washing facilities were similar to a concrete gent's type stall in the yard, with only cold water to wash in!

The next morning, we emerged from our freezing bedrooms and entered the dining room. All that was available for breakfast was a hardboiled egg, and only one per person! Oh, the glamour of show business!

Another band I knew worked the clubs in the Reeperbhan in Hamburg. In the cupboard, which passed as a dressing room and dormitory, of one particular club, there was a square metal cover over the top bunk bed. High, and merry after a show, one of the band tried to unscrew the bolts holding the plate to the wall. Suddenly a brown smelly liquid gushed over the bed and began to fill the dressing room! They had inadvertently unscrewed the rodding plate off the sewer pipe from the club's toilets leading to the outside drain! Talk about stink!! The lads could never recount that tale without heaving!

I am not the sort of person who is 'star struck', so I never really made the most of the opportunities to collect autographs and photographs - I wish I had. We must remember that today we can take a photograph from our phone, and modern digital cameras will fit into your pocket. Unlike their comparatively large and bulky predecessors, which had to be set up with flash and all the gear in order to get the elusive picture. I have tried to treat show business as just a job; albeit an exciting one, but there's not much glamour dragging your tired sorry ass up and down the country in the back of a Transit van! No, we shouldn't take ourselves too seriously, and we should not put ourselves above others - although a lot of show business people who I've met do have huge egos. When you are young, or things are going well, we humans have a tendency to think that it will always be that way - how foolish we are. Show business does strange things to people. After a bit of recognition, some people suddenly think they are stars, or the strain freaks out their minds and they feel that they must 'sparkle' twenty four hours a day. Sadly, there is always someone in the shadows with the means to help them achieve this.

I worked for a short while, attempting to get a set together, with a young man who had recently returned from a series of gigs in Acapulco, Mexico. He had just been sent back to the U.K. after being discharged from hospital. In the middle of a tour he had woken up one morning and suddenly imagined that he was Jesus! He dressed in a kaftan, threw off his shoes and paraded around the city streets barefoot - whilst playing a Spanish guitar! What made it worse, was that the little children began to follow behind him everywhere he went, only adding to the delusion. Thankfully, some months later he was able to laugh about it, but it's strange the things that lack of sleep and rest can do to the mind.

Addictions can easily become part of the performer's life. I knew a great guitarist who, in trying to stop smoking, had become addicted to Nicorette gum. He would not go on stage without a mouthful of the stuff, and always had several packets concealed about his person.

Overzealous fans can be difficult to handle too. One

young man surrounded himself with sycophants and smoked inordinate amounts of dope, given to him by his adoring fans; they thought that this was the way to his heart. He ended up totally incoherent, with bloodshot, streaming eyes and all he could utter was 'Nice man, nice.' If you asked him a question such as, 'How are things going?' 'Getting plenty of work?' all you got was, 'Yes man, nice, nice.' As he said these words he was constantly striking you with two large woollen pom-poms - the sort you would have on a knitted woolly hat - but these were about 100mm in diameter and connected by a short length of wool. As he spoke, the balls would bounce off your cheeks or the top of your head, very gently.

There was a vocalist called 'Cisco,' a really nice bloke. He always carried a microphone in his pocket (yes, it was just a microphone), in case he had to prove he really was a vocalist. In an attempt to impress the girls, he would unsheathe the mike, hold it to his mouth and sing something like, 'Stand By Me' into it. Those ladies who didn't walk off giggling were fair game. Still, it's better than the pratt of a singer who, after being accepted by an American rock outfit, was off to the States to fulfil a tour. In a nightclub called the Lafayette in Wolverhampton, he had the gall to tell me, 'Pete, we're all stars, but some of us shine brighter than others,' cheeky bastard! I never saw or heard of him again.

One of the saddest things now is that when I meet younger

ones stepping out on their careers, they don't seem to recognise that we older ones have a past. Although I'm now beginning to look like Father Christmas, I still have my moments! I always found, when in my youth, that if I met an old timer I would ask them questions - it's the only way to learn. Once in Liverpool, whilst sitting on a bench overlooking the river Mersey, I met a dear old lady who asked me what I was doing visiting the city. When I told her that I was with a band and about to embark on the Royal Iris, she began to tell me that when she was young she used to be in the chorus line at the Tower Theatre in New Brighton; it was a delight to hear her talk of the shows from those days. Even in the 1950's and 60's, New Brighton had a thriving fun fair and entertainment complex. Another casualty of both recession and peoples' holiday destinations changing, it was sadly left to run down, but thankfully I hear there are now plans to redevelop the area.

Another musician, who was a great storyteller, was a man named Tommy Blower - you remember, Tom was the labourer at the firm where I started as an apprentice in the tool room. Tom had a 'lived in' face and the laugh of an old pirate. In his youth he had played drums (not another one again), in the days of the big dance bands and had played for some well known bandleaders and at some famous venues. He used to regale me with stories of beautiful ladies gliding down wide Hollywood stairs, and having nothing on but see-through chiffon and a smile, ooh lovely! His nickname was 'Tiger,' because he was well known for his drumming solo in 'Tiger Rag.' Tom was a happy man. He used to bicycle to work and carried two tyre irons in his bag in case of a puncture. As he pulled off his cycle clips and walked through the door to clock in, he would drum with the tyre irons all along the wall and work benches, finally finishing with a flurry as the 'ding' of the clocking in bell marked his time card! Tom was a real old trouper and was always encouraging. He continued playing semi-professionally virtually up until the day he died.

I have worked with some big names who were very amateurish. At one very large venue, a particular lead guitarist was begging strings and a plectrum from me before the show started. I also worked, at the Civic Hall in Wolverhampton, with the ex-bass player of a three piece supergroup of the time, who had just formed his own group. I had admired him since my early school days, but what a letdown - he was so high, he couldn't tune his guitar properly! This sort of unprofessionalism only made us even more resolved to put on the best show we could, and prove that we should have been top of the bill.

I have worked with a few really miserable ones too; the sort who had done a bit of telly in the past. Sadly, some of them carried a chip on their shoulder, now that they were not stars anymore, and got easily narked when they couldn't have things their way. I always found this sort of person to be the most ungenerous and selfish. Or, there were the sort who latched on to someone else's shirt tails and told all who would listen how they knew so and so - attempting to bask in reflected glory. I did feel sorry for the old variety acts though; their world came crashing down quite quickly as the beat groups began to emerge, and I met a few folk who, because of this, had taken to the bottle.

I knew one old timer who did an audition for Hughie Green's 'Opportunity Knocks' and was surprised to be shown the door because he started a monologue about a man with a slot in his head (this had been his party piece from before the war which was really eluding to a penis!) When he related the story to me months later, he was still upset and shocked that no one would listen to him, he couldn't understand it - and he hadn't a good word to say about poor Hughie.

At some large dancehalls where we played, there were still part of the stage set ups around which the Big Bands used to use, you know, those boards that each musician sat behind, which had the name of the band painted on them. Sadly, most were covered in dust cloths, or just left as they were, piled in a corner or left languishing in a back room.

I went to see Tiger Tom at a working men's club on one occasion. He was drumming for an old pianist lady; she must have been nearly eighty years of age then, with pencilled on eyebrows and cupid bow painted bright red lips. I upset a few of her adoring fans when they noticed my broad smile, and hanky being stuffed into my mouth! Poor Tom almost exploded trying to keep his composure, tears ran down his laughter lines. After an excruciating few minutes trying to hold in my laughter, I waved him goodnight - the last I saw of him was his broad smile as he shook his fist at me! To dear Tom it was just another job.

Here are a few autographs of some of the beautiful people we had the privilege of working with. I didn't collect many, and I wish now that I had been more aware of the importance of the careers of the people we met, but as I said earlier, when you are young, you think that it is going to last forever and the people you admire will be around forever also - sadly that is not the case.

The expression 'worked with' is the term artistes use when they mean that they have performed on the same bill or at the same function. I have to say that it was a real thrill to meet someone who one really admired, even more so if the person came up to the expectations of the audience and behaved as a true lady or gentleman and professional. As a kid and upcoming performer, I will never forget the simple good manners and encouragement that was given to me by these wonderful people. It costs nothing to be nice, but believe me, it's never forgotten.

Authors Collection

The wonderful Esther Marrow. We met Queen Esther when she came to the UK as part of the Four Tops tour. Her mother named her Queen, and her career began when she was discovered by Duke Ellington. She has performed in front of Kings, Queens and Presidents and is currently the voice of the Harlem Gospel Singers.

A fabulous act we worked with in Birmingham was the great J.J. Jackson, perhaps you will notice his name on one of the posters.

Authors Collection

J.J. was a big man, weighing in at around 300 pounds or so. He wore a sparkling white suit and performed in the style of Otis Redding. He came to the UK in about 1966 and had a big hit with a song called, 'But It's Alright.' The band that night was truly awesome, being made up of some of Britain's finest jazz musicians. It was so exciting to see him interviewed on the early evening regional television, only to know that we would be performing with him later on that same evening!

At the time of appearing in the UK, Joyce had several hits and was well known on the Northern Soul circuit

Authors Collection

I particularly enjoy the reggae version of Kris Kristofferson's, 'Help Me Make it Through the Night,' and a wonderful song, 'Suddenly.' As I recall it was a great show.

Levi Stubbs of the Four Tops (nuff said, the best!)

Actually, we met Levi in Wolverhampton of all places, and at his request, performed as he danced those famous steps. He was an elegant mover and I consider him to be a gentleman, and rarely for so big a star, a humble man. As he himself said to me, 'I don't really have a style, Bill, when I sing I just give it the best I can.' Those words have always stuck with me; I was proud to have met him.

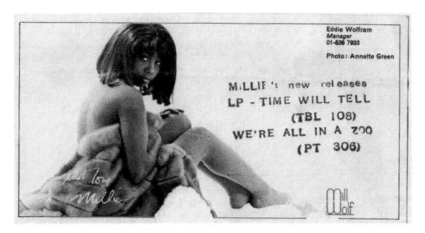

Eddie Wolfram
Manager
01-636 7933

Photo: Annette Green

M.LLIE 's new releases
LP - TIME WILL TELL
(TBL 108)
WE'RE ALL IN A ZOO
(PT 306)

Authors Collection

Millie was brought to the UK from Jamaica by Chris Blackwell in 1963, but sadly, by the time we worked with Millie, it's fair to say that she had never followed up on the success of 'My Boy Lollipop,' which was considered a novelty record at the time. She had so much more to offer. She was nevertheless professional and entertaining and a lovely girl.

Scene Six

Every silver lining has a cloud

I've always tried to do my very best to entertain the people who spend their hard earned money and come to see me in a show; as professionals we owe it to them .... but, giving of your all can be exhausting and tiredness can kill!

As a working band, we were constantly travelling from one end of the country to the other, starting early and getting home late - or should it be, starting late and getting home in the early hours. Many violent incidents in the night clubs, excess alcohol, poor diet, lack of sleep and unloading and loading about two tons of gear every night, along with the exhausting performances, were, unbeknown to me, taking a heavy toll on my mind and body.

I recall one time that in the early hours we had a puncture coming from a gig in the North of England. We were so tired and exhausted that we couldn't be bothered to look for the spare wheel and wrench. Partly dressed in stage clothes, we were standing in a semi-circle staring at the deflated tyre, when headlights pierced the darkness. The lorry driver that stopped must have wondered who on earth we were. There used to be a saying that lorry drivers were, 'The Knights of the Road.' This man certainly was. He saw the state we were in and offered to change the wheel and tyre for us. He would not accept a reward, truly a great human being. Added to this were a couple of incidents that brought me up sharp.

In 1985, Birmingham Handsworth saw terrible rioting. The tension had been building for many years due to police harassment, poor job prospects, colour prejudice and lack of opportunity for a growing disenfranchised generation of youth. (Thankfully, by 1985, I had left the band, so I was not around during these disturbances. By this time other wonderful outfits from Birmingham had begun to emerge, performing their own original edgy and exciting material.) However, during 1970/71 we happened to find ourselves in the middle of some frightening situations, possibly the start of the social upheaval that blossomed later in the 1980's, and I confess that, as a white man, a couple of times I thought I would not survive the night.

We emerged out of the Santa Rosa in the early hours of one Sunday morning and began to load the van. It was then that we became aware that the air was filled with smoke, there were blue flashing lights everywhere, the sound of breaking glass and the clamour of human voices and barking dogs was all around us. Once heard, the roar of an angry mob is never forgotten. Somebody, I don't know who to this day, pushed a flick knife into my hand and said, 'Use this if you have to!' I just stood there staring at it, wondering what on earth I was doing in this situation. I don't know who I was expected to use it on; I hardly shaved and couldn't stand the sight of my own blood, let alone anybody else's! Truth to tell, I was cacking myself! The police were, for the most part, white men, and I thought that the rioters may think me part of them. Bloody hell, I was just a musician - but an angry mob takes on a demonic quality and sees only what it wants to see! The boys who sometimes kindly helped us out, acting as 'roadies,' began to make weapons out of the microphone stands and anything else that came to hand. Police swarmed from everywhere. I don't know how, but after a few panicky moments, the lads bundled me into the van and ordered me to stay out of sight whilst they finished the loading.

We pulled off the car park and slowly weaved our way through an angry crowd and made our way down the Soho Road, eventually clearing the scene.

Just after that, another incident shocked me into realising that I had lost it. Whilst waiting to go on stage, in a show in Bradford I think it was, some young white English ladies came to invade the dressing room. I was feeling really ill and just wanted to sleep; I had consumed about a half bottle of rum and was in no mood for silliness. Some people may think that it's either funny or clever to speak in the 'patois' well, that is perfectly normal and understandable if a person's natural or mother tongue is spoken in that way, but most West Indian people who I have met, consider that a white youth speaking like this could well be perceived as showing disrespect. The young ladies happened to notice that I was rather quiet, and one of the silly half drunken girls enquired in the 'patois,' 'What is wrong widd de white boy?' I'm sorry, but I lost it. The flick knife handed to me in Handsworth that early morning was out of my travelling bag, open, and had not two of the boys been quick enough to wrestle me to the ground, would have been through her throat! Good God, I'd gone, I had flipped!

The boys were all getting stressed and the atmosphere began to become very strained between us; tempers could be lost quite easily, and from a happy little band we had become a miserable lot of bad tempered idiots.

I once saw a white youth, in a club in Huddersfield, speaking to two lovely West Indian girls using 'patois' garnished with dirty talk and swearwords. The young West Indian men in the club also overheard the dirty and disrespectful language and attacked the foolish youth with a view to seeing him off. It was then that the bravest door man I ever saw, shielded the fool with his own body, and thankfully saved his life. I really hope that we can respect each other's cultures, religions and ways of life - or things like this will happen. Everything makes for better relationships when basic good manners and decency rules are observed; I'm sure you agree. It's not to say that we can't have a smile about our differences, but let's be pleasant with each other.

There was a music shop which I used to frequent, Mel's Musical Exchange (nearly all musicians have a bolt hole like this). Some days later, I confessed to Mel about what had happened. By now I could not sleep through guilt and a feeling of stupidity over what could have been the outcome of my madness. Mel asked me for the knife and very kindly turned it in at the local police station. We need decent companions all the time, but particularly when our lives go belly up, and mine certainly was. I hear that Mel now has a very successful country and western act with a singer called Mary Lacey, I wish them well.

Another truly tragic incident began the final breakdown. I went to Willy's house early one Saturday afternoon. The idea was that we travelled together to meet with the rest of the boys, load the van and then journey on to perform a show in Leeds. One of Willy's children, five year old Andrew, wasn't feeling very well and was wrapped in a blanket on the sofa, watching the television. He had been diagnosed with measles. We said our farewells and as we went out of the door said we would see him later. Half way through the show, the police entered the club and asked to see Mr Williams. We were informed that Willie's wife and son were in hospital and that his wife had died, and we should head back to the Midlands immediately!

Without delay, in a state of shock and panic and working on autopilot, we hurried to pack up the equipment and get it into the van as quickly as possible. Hardly any words were spoken on the return journey. The police escorted us with blues and two's to the motorway and allowed us to speed back to the Midlands through the early hours. On arriving back, we went immediately to the hospital.

The police had got the message mixed up and confused. It wasn't Willy's wife who had died, but his little boy Andrew was now on a life support machine. It didn't look good. We had left him sleeping on the settee only hours before. After three days, the machine was turned off. He had passed away through meningitis and pneumonia brought on by the measles. A less impatient doctor could have possibly prevented this happening; had he simply done his job as a professional, perhaps being more observant in order to catch the infection in time, ... but apparently he was running late for a dinner date! I still think of Andrew. No words can express the devastation that was felt by Willy and his family.

Things were not really the same afterward, how could they be? As a travelling musician, leaving your family at home without you can create in one a feeling of guilt - the pleasure had now gone. I decided it was time to leave the band and was wondering how to break the news to the others, besides I was not feeling very well and guessed that something may be wrong. It was not long after the death of Andrew that Willy gave up drumming for good; he just walked out of the rehearsal room at the Y.M.C.A. and left the drums, still cased up in a pile in the corner. We still don't know what happened to them.

The storm broke.

In the early hours, on returning home from a gig, I began to shake violently. I went to bed and tried to sleep, but it happened again and the doctor was called. In the front room of my parent's house he examined me, gave me a sedative, and ordered me to report the next morning to his surgery for a full examination. Dr Ahmed was working away quietly, and then he spoke. 'I don't know what on earth you have been up to young man, but unless you stop it immediately you will be dead in six months!' My world stopped! He said that I needed to rest. He prescribed powerful anti-depressant drugs which simply knocked me out.

My days as a band musician were over. I returned home and wept, my body and mind could not take the strain. I thought that my life was finished and I would never be able to perform again. At the age of twenty, I was a burned out cinder and it was many, many months before I could even look at the old guitar.

Let me not to the marriage of true minds

admit impediments. Love is not love

which alters when it alteration finds,

or bends with the remover to remove:

O no! It is an ever fix-ed mark

that looks on tempests and is never shaken;

It is the star to every wandering bark,

whose worth's unknown, although his height be taken.

Love's not Time's fool, though rosy lips and cheeks

within his bending sickle's compass come:

Love alters not with his brief hours and weeks

but bears it out even to the edge of doom.

If this be error and upon me proved,

I never writ, nor no man ever loved.

William Shakespeare

The Blue Birds (1965)
L-R, Roger, Lynton, Steryl (Willy), Steve, Kenneth.

How the years have flown, as seen in the photograph of the members of the Blue Birds, how young Willy looked. Lynton died of a brain tumour before his 21st birthday, as I remember he was a quiet, well mannered, really nice lad. Steve, who had a very fine voice, was constantly being arrested by the police and at times was hurt. He fancied himself a bit (don't all young men?) but this used to bring out the worst in some people, and make them jealous when they saw him surrounded by pretty girls...I don't know what happened to Kenneth.

Somewhat of the boys personalities can be seen in the first photograph taken outside the Y.M.C.A. Roger was always smartly dressed, I noticed that he wore spats, and by now had grown pork chop sideburns. Jimmy Bass loved his white shoes and had just purchased a new yellow Fender bass guitar. Lloyd was always smiling, but he was no fool, he saw things on the business side before the rest of us. (By the time we had realised what had been happening it was too late, we were broke and it appeared that we had been fleeced by one of our own members.) He used to close his eyes and drift off when he blew his solos. A man with a kind heart, who many years later lent his saxophone to a so called friend, who had said he just wanted to have a go and learn .... Lloyd never had it returned or saw it again. Jimmy the vocalist was a rare talent. To be fair, he did not have a memorable voice, but he could work a crowd like no one I have ever seen. The young ladies would scream when he appeared on stage and cry with him during the last ballad - he loved it.

The Reason Why

L-R, Pete 'Bill' Shakespear, age 17 (Lead Guitar), Steryl, 'Willy' Williams (Drums), Roger Osbourne (Rhythm Guitar), Jimmy Dunkley (Bass), Lloyd Letman (Saxophone), Jimmy McLaren (Vocals), standing

The Reason Why 1969
L-R, Roger, Bill, Jimmy,
Jimmy, Willy.
Seated, Eddie Brown.
(The marks on the
photograph are where the
boys autographed the back.)

APPEARING AT THE

SANTA ROSA CLUB

SATURDAY 7th MARCH

THE PIONEER FROM JAMAICA
WITH THE CARIBOUS AND COUNT FINE DISCO SHOW

FRIDAY 13th and SATURDAY 14th MARCH

LLOYD WILLIAMS
AND THE SOUL CARAVAN

SATURDAY 21st MARCH

J. J. JACKSON FROM AMERICA

SATURDAY 28th MARCH

ALSO APPEARING **PYRAMID**

SATURDAY 4th APRIL

JIMMY JAMES AND THE VAGABONDS

SATURDAY 11th APRIL

WAGES OF SIN

SATURDAY 18th APRIL

JACKIE EDWARD AND COUNT PRINCE MILLER

SATURDAY 25th APRIL

SIGHT AND SOUND

SATURDAY 2nd MAY

FREDDY MACK

ALSO APPEARING EVERY NIGHT FROM 8 P.M. – 2.30 A.M.

THE REASON WHY ★ THE LEMON CREAM ★ BONNY JACKSON
with **D. J. DISCO SHOW RAY DAY**

6 A, SOHO ROAD   TEL. 545 4573

65, HIMLEY ROAD,
DUDLEY,
Tel. 57077

52, BRETTELL STREET
DUDLEY.
Tel. 58243

Mr. BILLINGS & KIETH

SAYING

HELLO ! HELLO ! MUMS & DADS LADS & LASSIES

STOP . LOOK . LISTEN

WE INVITE YOU ALL TO SEE—

BLACKPOOL ILLUMINATIONS

AND AFTERWARDS A LUXURIOUS

DANCING CRUISE

DOWN THE MERSEY ON THE

ROYAL IRIS

ON SATURDAY, 27th SEPTEMBER 1969

Coach Leaves TOP CHURCH, DUDLEY at 12 noon
and from BLACKPOOL at 9 p.m.

FOR DANCING CRUISE

MUSIC PROVIDED BY A GREAT YOUNG GROUP

THE REASON WHY

AND

THE KINGSTON FRIENDLY CLUB SOUND

PLEASE PHONE OR CALL AT THE ABOVE ADDRESSES
BEFORE THE DATE WITH YOUR MONEY

PRICE COACH & SHIP 55/-   *Thank you*

BLACKPOOL ILLUMINATIONS

AND

A CRUISE DOWN THE MERSEY
ON THE LUXURIOUS ROYAL IRIS
on
SATURDAY, 27th SEPTEMBER, 1969

This fabulous Ship has a Dance Floor for 1,000 people.
Three Bars, and many more pleasant features
Coach leaves Birmingham at 12 midday for Blackpool
Illuminations, then to Liverpool, where we embark on
the Royal Iris at 10.30 p.m.

Music provided by THE REASON WHY, Dudley's young
Up-and-coming Group, and COUNT CALLIE SOUND

PRICE FOR COACH AND CRUISE — 55/-
Tickets from:
THE REASON WHY — MR. BROWN
143 THORNBRIDGE ROAD, HALEY HALL, DUDLEY
Telephone : Brierley Hill 78912

This photo was taken
before Lloyd left the
band.

Ballroom on the
'Royal Iris.'

★ Come Cruising

Wolverhampton, Birmingham and Manchester Challet

This Magnificent Ship has its Dancing Accomodation, Bars and Several other Pleasant Features.

relax & enjoy the pleasure of a cruising to the Isle of Man
on Monday, 27th July 1970

Returning The Following Day

Come with the most exciting Group *Jimmy Mack with The Reason Why*. The Fabulous *Duke Sonny of Birmingham and his Sound*.

Coaches Leaves: Birmingham, Smethwick, West Bromwich, Walsall, Dudley, Rugeley, Bilston, Wolverhampton, Wellington and Manchester at 4.00 a.m. reaching LIVERPOOL by 7.30 a.m., then we Board the Luxurious **SNAEFELL** to the attractions of the **Isle of Man** where you will enjoy the beautiful atmosphere and the welcome of the Lord Mayor and his Associates, and other officials including the Directors of the Shipping Co., Transport and the Palace Lido etc.

DANCING OPERATION

The Palace Lido will be open for Dancing at 1.00 p.m. Continued until 2.00 a.m. TUESDAY, 28th JULY 1970. There are Bars, Lounge, Bingo Games etc. Food can be obtained to your choice of Purchase.

Boat return from the ISLE of MAN at 2.30 a.m. on TUESDAY 28th 1970

Return Price £6 - 0 - 0 Per Person. Cover, Coaches, Boat and Dance

Tickets can be obtained by EASY PAYMENT IN ADVANCE INSTALMENT, you get your Ticket Immediately after making your Last Payment.

CLOSING DATE FOR PURCHASING TICKETS
30th JUNE 1970

SPECIAL TOURS COST 5/- AROUND THE ISLE CAN BE ARANGED TO VISIT :- **NORTH ISLAND, RAMSEY, THE FAMOUS T. T. CIRCUIT** and The **SNAEFELL MOUNTAIN**

No Party will be Allowed on Board without TICKETS

'Shakespear'

Jon Tame (Bass) Pete Shakespear (Vocals)

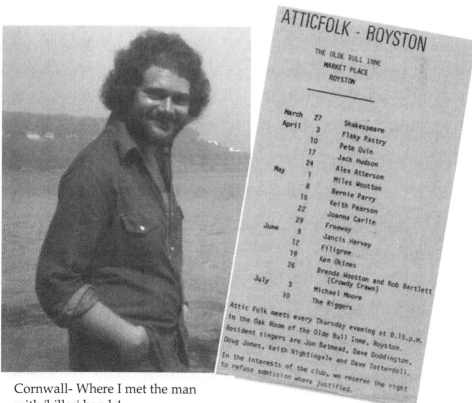

Cornwall- Where I met the man
with 'killer' hands!

ATTICFOLK - ROYSTON

THE OLDE BULL INNE
MARKET PLACE
ROYSTON

March	27	Shakespeare
April	3	Flaky Pastry
	10	Pete Quin
	17	Jack Hudson
	24	Alex Atterson
May	1	Miles Wootton
	8	Bernie Parry
	15	Keith Pearson
	22	Joanna Carlin
	29	Freeway
June	5	Jancis Harvey
	12	Filigree
	19	Ken Okines
	26	Brenda Wootton and Rob Bartlett (Crowdy Crawn)
July	3	Michael Moore
	10	The Riggers

Attic Folk meets every Thursday evening at 8.15.p.m.
in the Oak Room of the Olde Bull Inne, Royston.
Resident singers are Jon Betmead, Dave Doddington,
Doug Jones, Keith Nightingale and Dave Totterdell.
In the interests of the club, we reserve the right
to refuse admission where justified.

The album 'Stay with Shakespear' (RR2001).

The musicians on the session were: the brilliant Ken Price on guitar and harmony vocals, Dave 'Biffo' Griffiths, bongos and tambourine and Paul Millman on drums.

40 years later, still available from Accoustic Soup Rare Records.

RECORDED AT: Mid Wales Sound Studios
ENGINEERED BY: Alan Green
PRODUCED BY: Gordon Davies

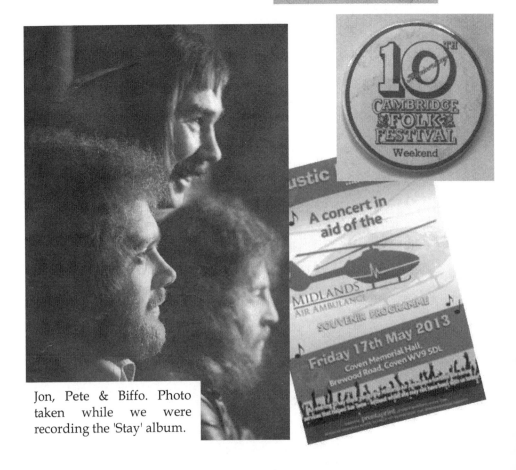

Jon, Pete & Biffo. Photo taken while we were recording the 'Stay' album.

Pete (Bill) and Steryl (Willy) one last time at Steryl and Molly's 40th wedding anniversary.

ACT TWO

Scene One

Facing the devil

The months ahead were just a daze and feeling ill. I found myself drifting in and out of consciousness and half reality - boy those drugs smacked me! I didn't have the strength to do anything, all my energy was gone; I didn't want to eat or wash and I was becoming a tramp. Left alone in my room I just slept. I lost complete contact with the outside world. I guess the other members of the band thought I must be OK, and so no one bothered to seek me out. I never saw them as a group again. It's quite easy to stay in touch, but maybe some in the band thought I had dropped out on purpose. Not long after I was forced to leave, Willy himself left; maybe the rest of the band thought that we had colluded, I don't know. Even now, today, I find a lot of people I've known over the years to be shallow, only seeming to want to be around when things are going well. True friends are like gold and should be treasured.

Then came the panic attacks. I would not wish those on anyone. You feel as though you just want to run, as if the devil himself was after you; in reality this is your own imagination, but something sparked the attacks off. I had seen enough fighting, blood, stabbing and nastiness to last a lifetime; the crazy thing is, if you are a sensitive person, you can't easily get the pictures out of your mind.

At home, where I lived with my parents, the atmosphere was always one of great tension, and growing up with this state of affairs was not easy. It was another reason for me to try and break away. I am afraid to say that my father could be a violent, moody and insensitive man when he chose to be, and had little regard for my mother when it came to using his fists. Neighbours too, sometimes got caught out with his moods. I thought I had escaped the difficult situations which could arise in having to placate another human being, in case you looked at him the wrong way, or happened to say the wrong thing, ... but I hadn't. My childhood had been fraught with anguish; I now found myself once again in the lion's den. This time I could see no way out, and I must confess, that at one point I considered the unthinkable!

The bad memories were hard to handle. What can a little child do when both parents are holding knives, about to cut each other? They begin to grapple; my father gets my mother in a headlock and cuts her forehead with the breadknife, ... blood oozes out. Even, long before he died, Granddad told them,

'You two fight like cat and dog!'

But everybody turned a blind eye. Who on God's earth could stop them? As a result of the strain, I began to suffer the most horrendous nose bleeds. I am afraid that for a little lad I was a bit of a wreck! It's amazing the hold parents like this can have on their children, and they are so clever at hiding their behaviour from other members of the family, like aunts and uncles, who even today, do not want to talk about it. Incidents like this happened with regularity and it began to create problems for me at school.

The math's teacher at the time was a witch named Mrs Lee. Because I could not concentrate, she would scream, not only at me, but at the other kids who were in her opinion too slow. We were, 'A lot of morons, numbskulls and thick!!!' Her screaming voice could be heard a mile away across the village. What a waste of space this sort of teacher was. My heart goes out to any young person who has to suffer this kind of existence.

I now find it strange that a man like my father, who could turn violent so quickly, could also behave like a saint; after all, how does one explain the wonderful and touching example of humanity shown to Albert. Albert was a friend of my grandfather. Together, they had fought with the marines in France during the First World War, where my grandfather had been severely wounded. The marine regiments were formed from the ranks of trained navy sailors when there was a shortage of warships, and the army needed more cannon fodder for the trenches. Thus Albert and my grandfather entered the fray at the battle of Cambrai on the Western front; my grandfather's war finishing abruptly on 30th December 1917, at the action at Welch Ridge.

The war played awful games with these men's minds, and together with the actions and empty promises of the government of the day, these brave men became very bitter. They were promised a land fit for heroes. Sad really, that after spending seven million pounds a day attempting to defeat the Germans (in what was really a royal family argument about two spoilt brats wanting their own ships), the donkeys couldn't even find the proud returning lions a job, let alone good housing, and the poor heroes had to virtually grovel for assistance to maintain any vestige of dignity. If it wasn't for the charitable good works of women like Mrs Hawkesford and Mrs Jacques, encouraging the old soldiers to seek help, I dread to think how they would have fared.

Albert would not be seen for months, but eventually he would turn up out of the blue at my grandfather's house and stay for a few days. During his stay he would shave off his long red beard and smarten himself up; but Albert had the wanderlust, as granddad called it, and would soon disappear again. Through his experiences in the Great War, he could not settle, and spent many months each year living as a 'gentleman of the road.' My father worked in the building trade, employed as a pipe layer, scaffold erector and general labourer. So it was that early one morning, whilst cycling on his way to work, he noticed Albert living rough under a hedge and stopped for a while. On seeing Albert's predicament, without hesitation, he gave him his own day's breakfast and lunch sandwiches. My father would then have gone hungry, working a hard and long shift, rather than see Albert suffer. How do you account for a wonderful deed like that? Compassion on one hand, and rage on the other!

Whilst going through some papers that were left to me from my father's estate, I came across a letter addressed to my grandfather from the Government. It read, 'Your request for a winter overcoat has been refused.' The poor man - he, like many thousands, was left to rot after he had almost lost his life in a war, defending what he felt was a way of life and system that he believed in. The wounds eventually did kill him, but many years later, after a lifetime of suffering. He died alone and was found sitting in an armchair, still leaning on his walking stick. The doctor said that he died with his boots on, good old granddad! Truth to tell, if he were alive today, the chances of him or his generation being able to walk the streets of England freely, without being mugged, would probably be very slim. As a society what a legacy we have created, where regard and respect for each other has all but vanished. Perhaps this is what made my father dislike authority so much; seeing his brave old dad and his comrades treated as of no account and with such disrespect. I suspect he thought a musician's life was a bit 'soft' and probably he wanted me to be more 'manly,' anyway we didn't really see eye to eye or communicate much, and for the most part went our separate ways. The rest of the family too thought that I was a bit 'funny,' especially after being ill. After all, a life in show business was not the norm among working class people; the building site or factory was the expected way to earn a living. I however, always wanted more, and felt devastated now that my mind and body had let me down. In this lonely world I had to survive, I could not tell anyone what the group had been through, the bad or the good times. The family just knew that I played in a band and sometimes didn't come home - and now something had happened to me. In my heightened state, I guess all the pent up stress of the past twenty years came to a head and acted as a catalyst to expose the burden that I had carried since childhood.

In this day and age all forms of abuse are openly spoken of, but back then, a lot of lads had violent fathers and we all just got on with it. On several occasions, when it was really bad, if one tried to intercede between my mother and father during a violent row, they would join forces and you could find yourself being attacked by both of them, either verbally or physically! I think mother took some perverse delight in having a black eye; still I suppose it's a good excuse to tell others that you bumped into a door! My immediate family and relatives failed to really understand why I didn't attend my parents' funerals, although it was totally by accident that I learned of both their passing, due to spitefulness and suspicion from family members. The past is best buried along with the sad memories.

It's fair to say that poverty was rampant in certain streets and areas of every town and village, even during the 1950's. It got too much for at least two of the fathers of children who I went to primary school with; they simply lay down on a cushion on the kitchen floor, stuck their heads into a gas oven, turned on the tap, and went to sleep. The unlit coal gas in those days could kill very effectively if you breathed it in. The streets were still lit by gas lamp. A man on a bicycle would move from lamp to lamp turning on the light using a long pole. Even some homes were still without electricity and had to rely on gas for their lighting. Our house too was lit by gas - once, I remember, I had to run down to Mr Thomas' hardware store and buy new gas mantles! In the scullery there was only one cold water tap above an old Belfast sink. A large black coal range was the only means of heating. When electricity was eventually fitted by the council and we needed a new light bulb (yes, there was only one electric light in the house until some years later,) once again I was down to the hardware store, this time Mr Thomas enquired who I was. I replied by giving my name and where I lived, he said that he knew the name and asked me the Christian name of my granddad. Mr Thomas said he was in the trenches in France with granddad and if there was anything that we wanted we only had to ask; he even offered to fit the light bulb for us! That community spirit has long disappeared and working class people seem to have forgotten that almost everybody was in the same boat at one time.

Materialism began to rear its ugly head as the 1960's saw better times for working people. The Prime Minister of the time had the audacity to tell the British people that they had never had it so good, cheeky bugger! He was probably right, but he didn't need to rub their bloody noses in it! You knew something was coming when you overheard one woman ask another;

'You have a washing machine don't you?'

'Yes, you're not having one are you?'

'Yes.'

'Oh I have a so and so make, the best ....' and so it went on. People in the factory would let it out that they were having a new fitted carpet from Cyril Lord, perhaps one of the first carpet companies to advertise on television, or they would offer to let you 'jump in the car' or knowingly ask,

'Have you ever been to such and such?' - a seaside resort or some other place. All designed to let you know that they were showing off and were attempting to throw off the working class mantle. It only got worse when package holidays began to grow; now it was Spain that they began to brag about. I've lost count of the number of kids who knew Wales like the back of their hand or could speak fluent Spanish at the age of ten! The family of one of my school friends moved out of their council rented terraced property, to a newly-built council three bedroom semi-detached. His mother began to speak differently, and have her hair coloured with a blue rinse, no kidding, Mrs Bucket did exist.

Many years later I knew a man who had been a crooner in the 1950's and fancied himself as a cut above. He won a competition to have a short flight on Concord and thought that he had made it. One day, during a conversation with our crooner friend and a company pilot that I knew quite well, he began to pontificate about the mystique of flight and glow with pride about his free trip on Concord. To attempt a piece of 'one-upmanship,' he turned to me and asked,

'Have you ever flown, Pete?'

I replied cheekily, 'I had a kite once!'

The pilot winked and laughed heartily, but crooner's face showed disdain, I hadn't the heart to tell him that I had taken the stick of a small aircraft on many occasions from a little airfield near Wolverhampton. What a silly man! It was the same bloke who simply had to have the biggest new car for both himself and his wife. Unfortunately, he died unexpectedly, and it was then discovered that he owed so much money that the house had to be repossessed, leaving his wife homeless. The poor woman had been oblivious to the fact that he hadn't two brass farthings to rub together. So much for showing off! As a result of seeing such foolishness at first hand, I am afraid I can't stand materialism. It's good to work hard and prosper, but not to flaunt your showy display of your means of life in front of others, who may not be as fortunate as you are.

As a kid I used to dread the winters. 1963 saw a particularly bad one, and with my father being laid off from his job on the building site, because of the low temperatures and the depth of snow, we had it rough. That winter was extreme, the nation virtually ground to a standstill, even trains had to be dug out by hand because of the drifting snow. We lived on beans on toast for three months, well, it felt like it! The pipes would freeze to the outside privy, then burst when it thawed, and snow would be blown in through the gaps in the bedroom windows. There was no such thing as central heating, and it was really bad if you happened to pull the arm off the eiderdown!! Nobody had much really, but some kids had no shoes and socks! Yes, I know it was the late 1950's and early 1960's, but the slum clearances were just getting under way and if you were silly enough to give your meagre weekly wage to the bookie, pub landlord or Mr Woodbine, then you were destined not to have much. If you were unskilled and lacked education it could be hard, and working men were treated like cattle to be hired and fired at will. What's changed? My other grandfather Bill, a skilled engineer and welder, who in the 1930's found work in the shipyard at John Brown's in Glasgow working on the Queen Mary, told me he used to dye his hair with gravy browning; the old ones got it in the neck first, so they all tried to stay as young looking as possible. I eventually did break out, although, breaking away from the pack is tough. Once you move on, you are not accepted back, so you need to keep moving forward - there's no other place to go! Never let the pack hold you back, just go for it! I wanted more, not as an insult to my parents, but I knew there was more to life than struggling in the factory or being on a building site in all weathers. I heard on the B.B.C., during an interview programme, how apparently some years ago, Randy Newman, the wonderful singer songwriter, was having a good moan one day about how he had not had a hit for a while. His brother was a building worker at the time and told him to shut up, what he had got was better than threading pipe. What a lesson for all of us.

I worked on a show in the U.K. with a really humble old negro blues man one time. To my absolute shame I have forgotten his name. He told me that in his home in the U.S., he got a job opening the show for a really successful and famous blues legend. He related the story to me of how he arrived at the gig in an old beaten up Ford pickup and pulled it round the back of the venue. He took his old scratched guitar from the back seat, adjusted his boiler suit, and knocking the dust off his clothes and shoes entered the dressing room. The famous man appeared in front of the building in a brand new Cadillac with two bodyguards. He was dressed in a beautiful white suit and was well covered in bling, gold bangles and chains. My old blues friend, relating the story said,

'And you know the first song the star sang? Yes sir, a blues called, 'Hard Times!'

He only smiled and shook his head, but you get the picture.

All the years of trying to cope with my parents, finally came to a head some years later, when my own son was born. Over the years I had made an effort to overlook their imperfections, blaming it on poverty and a lack of education, or perhaps they didn't understand my personality, after all, show business does make you a bit different, but I always attempted to see the best in people. Like most young families, a visit to the parents on a Sunday afternoon to take the children was the norm, and I thought that by showing kindness we would get close enough to enable us to talk about matters and repair broken bridges. This was not to be, my father started to belittle me in front of my child. That was enough. I was not going to allow his brand of sarcasm to affect another generation. Suffice to say that I walked out of their lives. It is no good wishing things were different; there would be no reconciliation, I now knew that it would never be - so I moved on. My father died a few years ago, my mother quite recently. I only heard about my father's death when someone suggested I visit the hatched, matched and despatched website of a local newspaper; none of the rest of my family could be bothered to tell me. Some years later the same thing happened after I had heard my mother had been admitted to hospital, I was informed that she was ill, she passed away within days. No one telephoned to tell me about the funeral. It happened again when I found out by accident that my uncle John had died. Sadly, most of my relatives still don't understand my decision to distance myself, and that anyway, they say, I was always a big head! What a legacy.

When I met the girl who was later to be my wife, I vowed that I would never allow that kind of bickering and falling out in our house, and I have passed that rule on to my son. Suffice to say that we are all very close, and that's the way it should be isn't it? I still have off days, but I always bounce back after counting my blessings.

At Mel's Musical Exchange, the music shop where I sometimes hung out, a couple of lads called in one day to do some business and over a cup of coffee, asked me to join them for a musical get together at their favourite watering hole. Here I could just listen if I wanted to and not get too involved, just turn up and have a smile and be made welcome.

The establishment was the Plough Inn at Willenhall, the

town where I had first heard great live music. Among the crowd that frequented 'The Plough,' were a number of 'drug experts.' After a few visits to the Plough, the lads got to know me better and we began to relax in each other's company. When I explained my circumstances, they asked what I was taking for my problem. On showing them the little bottle, with my daily supply of capsules, their eyes bulged! They offered to buy all I could supply! I wondered why there was such an interest in what I considered to be the devil's sweets; I hated these things that had turned me into a zombie.

'Where did you get these?'

'From the Doc,' I said.

'Great gear man, how many are you on?'

'Six a day,' said I.

Looking shocked, an older man exclaimed,

'Good God man, just one of these would stop a racehorse!' Now this explained why I couldn't bother to wash or eat, write or play anymore, like I said, I had become a zombie and I wouldn't wish it on anyone. I would not sell my supply, I couldn't. I knew then that I was addicted and had become dependent on this awful drug. Everywhere I went I always carried a little plastic bottle of my little helpers; I would not move from the house without them. As you can imagine, life at this time was very difficult. But being befriended by the boys at the Plough probably saved my life. I have to say that these lads were the best medicine and tonic I could have wished for. They were kind, hospitable and sharing, and I feel they took me to their hearts. They encouraged me to play a few chords, and slowly, I began to involve myself in the musical evenings at the pub. There are so many stories to come out of the good times of laughter and merriment spent at 'The Plough,' that it would take another book to tell them all, however, I will relate a couple of tales that I still titter at to this day.

The boys decided to have a party for Christmas and one of them, Martin, I think it was, made an old wellington boot fit onto a two by two piece of wood. Bottle tops were nailed on to the wood; this made a jingly jangly sound as the boot was thumped on the floor, and was to provide a 'percussion' accompaniment to the guitarists - me and a bloke called Tona. As the evening wore on, different people would be allowed to have a go at playing the welly. A good time was being had by all. The noise of the singing happy crowd could be heard across the town. Eventually, the music became louder as we turned up the volume to compete with the crowd. The valves on the little Linear amp were glowing blue! We didn't care, and it was becoming a 'happening' good night! It became even more raucous as the welly began to beat out the rhythm of the music on the light fittings! By the time someone called a halt to the proceedings, the light fittings were completely flattened against the wall; we must have gone mad. The landlord was found collapsed behind the bar well smashed, and beer was running through the open door and into the pavement gutter outside. The landlord's wife was perched on a bar stool, glassy eyed and singing happily to herself, tears running down her face; she was lovingly holding onto a bottle of something strong! Everybody had gone OTT, but that night happiness exuded out of the Plough!

Another night, a man who had imbibed a bit too much, began to take offence at the antics of Tona, who after a gym session was flexing his pectoral muscles and making the wings flap of an eagle tattooed on his chest. In an effort to compete, the silly old fool ripped his threadbare vest from the neck down, to reveal his flabby torso. After regaining their composure, I am afraid that the lads tore at the rest of his worn and smelly clothes and threw them on to the open coal fire! The clown fled from the building half naked, farting into the night air outside, clutching his hands around his private parts! It was the same fireplace, that when things went a bit quiet, someone would throw fireworks into the coals - one time blowing the fireplace off its fixings!

The boys decided one evening to put on a small party for a couple of old age pensioners who were regulars in the snug. They were the sort of folks who could make a bottle of brown ale last all night, nevertheless, they were quiet and usually friendly. This party night, the couple, Flo and Charlie, were celebrating their wedding anniversary. We played old rock and roll tunes and sentimental ballads from the 1950's especially rehearsed for them. One of the wags, unbeknown to them or us, had a beautifully iced cake made for the occasion. It had on it a few candles and was set on a silver base, but under all the trimmings, the cake was made of wood! The evening was growing late and after much ale had been imbibed by all, one of the lads asked that the cake be presented to them. The happy pair had been eulogising about how wonderful the boys were for thinking of them on this special occasion. Saying 'There the best set of lads anywhere in the world, and they were very lucky to have found such wonderful friends.'

Billy, wearing a broad smile, asked for a chair to be brought out. To a great cheer, he promptly lifted Flo on to it and asked her to make a speech. Meanwhile her husband, although old, was still a big man, about six foot six tall and weighing in at around twenty stones or so, and he began to weep at the beauty of the occasion. He was shaking everybody's hand and wishing them all good health and happiness. A large kitchen knife was handed to Charlie and he was asked to cut the cake.

'Cut the cake, cut the cake!' everyone shouted in chorus.

With his wife holding the cake and standing on the chair, surrounded by a grinning and smiling crowd, he plunged the knife into the middle of the beautifully iced confection. The knife stuck, it could not be removed! He desperately attempted to extricate the blade, pulling and twisting, first one way then the other, and in his vain attempt, almost pulled his wife off the chair! She stopped crying, his face hardened, they both realised about the same time that they had been had! The cake, still with the knife firmly embedded in it, flew through the air. Suddenly these wonderful friends were the, 'Biggest bastard scumbags anyone could know!' and a scuffle broke out.

Everyone fell about helplessly laughing. The long suffering constabulary were always popping in and warning that the establishment would be closed down if things carried on like this. One night, the News of The World sent a reporter and photographer to interview Tona, who had convinced them that he was the new Bob Dylan! My cheeks and stomach used to ache from laughing. I have never had so much fun before or since. I began to realise now, that if you work hard then you must play hard, and always find time for a smile. I don't take myself too seriously these days, although if someone thinks me a fool I can bite if I have to, but that's rare, I try to keep as my friends those who are able to laugh at themselves and are self deprecating.

On a visit to 'the smoke,' it was arranged by the lads that in exchange for free beer, I would play in the bar of the Chelsea Potter public house on the Kings Road during Sunday lunchtime. This was OK, but the holed and patched jeans I was wearing attracted the attention of a bloke who offered me a substantial sum to take them off! No not that way! He wanted to buy them there and then; I don't know what he thought I was going to wear, but this was the source of much amusement. This gig didn't last for long, within weeks the then landlord disappeared with the contents of the till! By the time the staff opened the bar on Monday morning he had done a moonlight. Whether he was ever found I don't know, but we enjoyed the gig while it lasted. On this same trip, going through London, we were all sitting in the back of a tipper lorry driven by an acquaintance of Tona's, Bob from Doncaster. When Tona spotted a tow rope in the corner of the wagon floor, he had what started off as an innocent idea. Standing up, he began to swing it around his head in cowboy fashion, showing off and whooping loudly. It unfortunately slipped through his fingers, and as he let go, it lassoed a man in a petrol station who had stopped to fill his car with fuel! The lorry screeched to an abrupt halt and we all leapt down off the tailgate. Everyone apologised to the man, and after shaking hands and making an offer to contribute to his petrol bill, we mounted the lorry to continue on our merry way. As the lorry drew away again, we wet ourselves with laughing, picturing the shocked look on the poor chap's face. Oh boy that could have been nasty, but it was only devilment, not maliciousness. Anything for a laugh, not nastiness, was the way the boys thought - and life was fun.

I will be forever indebted to Tona, Kipper, Scobi, Bill and the others for such a happy period in my life.

Bryan appeared at my parent's house one day and said he was a writer; he had heard of me and wanted to know if we could put some stuff together. He had had some success with sending in jokes and writing short sketches for 'The Two Ronnies' and others. Although he wrote sketches and songs, he needed some new material and thought that maybe our collaboration would bring a new direction and impetus.

I had been working on a song called 'Stay,' and after finally completing the arrangement, we made a rough recording on an old reel to reel machine in Bryan's mother's garage. We caught the train to London and stayed overnight, sleeping on the floor at my Aunt Pauline's house in Maidenhead. We had a view to hawking the song around the major record companies. As you can imagine, arriving unannounced, we were thrown out of most of them. Some A&R men even used some well chosen Anglo Saxon phrases that should never be repeated, to ensure that we must never darken their doors again!! But we trudged on and eventually we gained an appointment at EMI. We were welcomed at the door by a commissionaire in uniform and escorted through the offices to a private room. Along the way we observed that the walls were covered in gold discs of all the great legends of the time. We were shown into a little office and invited to sit down. The man placed the tape reel on a machine, set up next to his desk. After a few minutes of listening, he exclaimed, 'Great song boys.' He disappeared into another office with the tape and we heard the song being played again. After what seemed an interminable wait, he returned and said,

'We would like to offer you a contract for all writing, performing, merchandising, everything - but we want you to perform as a duo,' - a sort of new 'Peter and Gordon.'

Bryan would not sign; he said he didn't want to perform, and would not sing! Once again I had backed the wrong horse. Unfortunately, in my state, I had not the confidence to see it through on my own, and anyway they wanted to market a duo.

Later we blagged an interview at 'Apple' in Savile Row; it was on the roof of this building that the Beatles performed for the last time. The office decor was a theme of pink flock wallpaper, pink leather chairs and pink telephones. The staff were encouraging and listened politely. It was very nice, but I don't think that we were really what they were looking for. I returned to the Midlands very sad and disappointed. Imagine my shock, when later I heard that the A&R executive at EMI, was none other than George Martin's right hand man at that time, Norman Smith, who later had a hit with 'Don't Let it Die' - I wished now that I had! Oh bugger. After that I just slipped into a great depression.

Bryan told me how he too had once been addicted to a tranquillizer and had weaned himself off them by breaking open the capsules, and over many months, gradually reducing the amount of white powder in them. I began to do the same and, thank God, a long period of recovery began.

As my head began to clear and as the months went by, I felt the urge to pick up my guitar and write again. I plonked through a few chords, but after a few minutes felt totally drained. I suppose though that making music is in the blood and I persevered.

Whilst strolling aimlessly around the shops one day, I discovered a health food store down by the market in Wolverhampton. After a chat with the owner, who had approached me as I wandered around the aisles, wondering if I felt alright (I must have looked like death warmed up), he suggested that I pursue an 'ultimate' nutrition programme of healthy eating and gentle exercise. I took his advice and began to take vitamins and supplements purchased from the shop, and after many months I began to feel better; but I still lacked the confidence that all entertainers must have, both to perform, and in their own abilities. My appearance was rather shabby too, a far cry from the days of mohair suits! I had fallen a long way, hadn't I?

Although the experience has been many years ago, I still have periods where all I want to do is live quietly. But, when I'm feeling chipper, my old friends still say that I am a bit larger than life; I don't mean to come over like that, it's just me. I do find though that aggressive and unthinking people are vexatious to the soul and if I can, I avoid them like the plague.

After what seemed an eternity, I now made up my mind to go back to my acoustic roots, and began to seek out suitable songs to perform and to build an entertaining set.

One afternoon I noticed that a little green sports car was parked outside the house. There was a knock at the door and on opening it, there stood a couple of likely lads - I seemed to attract them. The red haired boy introduced himself, 'I'm Pat and this is Wally.' Again from where they got my address I know not, but into my life came Wally the bin man, and Pat Hannon a works electrician and a truly talented man. The two wanted to form a harmony band. They were used to performing their own songs and covers of Bee Gees material. I said that I wasn't interested, but then one of them produced a guitar, and the two of them began to sing. The harmonies were stunning. The pair used to rehearse in the bathroom of Wally's flat. The tiled walls reflected the voices marvellously, although heaven knows what the neighbours thought. To this day, I say that Pat Hannon was one of the most versatile singers I have ever met, his range was unbelievable. Although nothing came of their attempt to entice me to join them, Pat and I eventually wrote quite a lot of material together, but a little more of Pat later.

Scene Two

<u>Three songs Pete</u>

An old pal of mine, an actor, trying to make his way in the profession, suggested that I take my guitar to a folk club which he knew of, and have a plonk as a floor singer. I hadn't been inside a folk club since my school days, but I trusted his judgement as a professional and decided to give it a try. After visiting quite a few clubs over a couple of months, to familiarise myself with the general arrangement of things, I began to rehearse some songs to get a set together.

One Saturday evening, I took the bull by the horns and bowled into 'The Three Stirrups' in Brewood and asked if a floor spot was available, to see if I could fit in. The club organiser, Pete Hancox, requested that I perform three songs, the usual number that newcomers were allowed. Well, I'd done it! I was in front of an audience again. I never really expected to enter the folk music world, but I enjoyed singing, and meeting really nice gentle people. I continued to visit a large number of clubs in the area performing three songs - albeit different ones each time - and because of this, some wag christened me, 'Three songs Pete!' After a while, I began to pick up engagements in my own right. People would approach me at a club and ask me to perform at another club as guest act, and sometimes even to sing at someone's wedding or social gathering. Once again I found myself moving in the circles of great musicians.

Most of the performers I met had to stand or fall, for the most part, without the backing of other musicians. This gave these great, talented people a confidence and independence that I admired. Now, once again, I began to meet some of my musical heroes. I enjoyed the performances of the great Alexis Korner. He was perhaps the founding father of British blues, and boy, did he have presence! Eventually, he achieved chart and television success, but for years played the blues clubs. I had a couple of knocks with Alexis in clubs in Wolverhampton and London. He wished me well and I appreciated that, he made me also promise to carry on with my adventure. Alex Campbell was truly a troubadour, and when he sang 'I've Been on the Road so Long,' the tears would roll down his cheeks. He used to say to me, when we had had a few drinks, 'Ah Wee Peter, you're gonna be a star!' How I miss him, he died some years ago - ah, if only his words had turned out to be right. I worked with a great blues man, although a lot of people probably wouldn't know this, it was Long John Baldry. He is probably best remembered for his great Number One, 'Let the Heartaches Begin,' but John could really play the blues. He was a tall man, over six feet, hence the name. He was so disgusted with himself at 'selling out,' that he said he would nail his gold disc for the song to the back of the toilet door! I don't know if he ever did, but again, it's a good story.

I first met Gerry Lockran at a club in Brewood in Staffordshire. In the early 1970s, he was managed by Nigel Thomas, who at that time represented Joe Cocker, The Grease Band, Rod Stewart and The Faces, Chris Stainton, Juicy Lucy and Alexis Korner. Gerry had not long finished a three month tour of the U.S. and Canada, involving some thirty or forty concerts, opening the show for Joe Cocker in the 'Mad Dogs and Englishmen' tour and he was on top form. We hit it off straight away, and whenever I wasn't working and Gerry was in town, we met for a Scotch or two. He was really amused when I said that I used to watch him on the telly. Gerry had been at it a long time and knew everybody in the business. As with all these other performers, he could hold an audience in the palm of his hand - what a professional. One night Gerry was appearing at The Victoria Hotel in Wolverhampton, and with an old pal from the Plough, Scobie, and a bloke nicknamed 'Fuzzy' Graham (because of his curly hair), I went along to see him. Incidentally, the Victoria Hotel had the best resident I ever saw in a folk club, Dave Start, a brilliant entertainer. Gerry went down a storm as always, and the crowd wanted him to carry on. He said that he had a train to catch to Euston and had to go ..... unless someone could give him a lift to London? He obviously never expected what happened next! Scobie leaned over to me and said, 'We will take him if he wants to stay a bit longer.' Gerry was pleasantly shocked, but the audience was delighted. On the way down to London on the M1 we played song after song, having a really good time. I remember he told me, 'You can't play a guitar man, but you have the best delivery in the business!' What a compliment from such a great trouper who had worked with the best.

A few weeks later, Gerry invited me to London to meet his management. Some studio time was arranged for me at Southern Music with a man named Bob Kingston. I asked my old writing partner, Pat Hannon to accompany me. Bob Kingston had arranged for a young producer, just starting out on his career, to take the session.

Colin Thurston was a brilliant engineer and producer, he went on to engineer for David Bowie and Duran Duran. We recorded four songs, 'Mr Nod,' 'Jeannie Come Home,' 'Standing on the Threshold of Heaven' and 'Lady Ann.' I did have the sessions on reel to reel, but somewhere they have been lost. I left a lot of stuff at my parent's house and I guess they were thrown out or destroyed, but if anyone has a copy please let me know.

Pat and I enjoyed our song writing and we had many a good, relaxing drinking session afterwards! He would pretend to be a ventriloquist, using a little flat capped dummy that he named 'Dick.' After a late night writing session, I would bunk down on the settee and he would leave me to sleep. I swear 'Dick the Dummy' could leave his nail on the wall and walk around the room. Well, not really, it was just Pat in the darkness attempting to scare me, but he could never hold his laughter in and would be heard giggling as 'Dick' crept up in the blackness of the room, whispering, 'I'm going to kill you!', until Pat fell over something in the dark, and 'Dick' would be returned to his nail! I wasn't aware of the toll that alcohol was taking on Pat until some years later.

We did a special gig together when a local Midland attraction was developing a new amusement area for children based on a 'Fairyland of Gnomes.' We wrote several songs about gnomes and Keith the manager of the 'Tandy' shop produced a looped tape which was to be played continuously through loudspeakers as background music for the attraction

(Some years later Keith went on to develop a very successful public address hire company.) When the venture came to be officially opened we were invited to perform our songs to a live audience.

On the opening night, the car park filled with Rolls-Royces and other prestige vehicles. Chauffeur driven magic carpets transported tuxedo dressed, dickey bowed, ball gowned and bejeweled dignitaries. Together with London bankers and the financial backers of the venture, they were to wine and dine the night away. The best Champagne was laid on and a red carpet was rolled out. The local press was assembled to interview and photograph the great and the good. We performed our live set under a massive crystal chandelier in a large marquee especially set up for the occasion. After a buffet meal and more Champagne, speeches, handshakes and more Champagne, the guests were invited to take their seats in the open coaches of a little steam train which had been especially set up to travel on a track weaving through the trees of the grounds. It was to be a mystery parcel hunt. At pre-selected points along the track, the train was to stop for the passengers to alight into the woods, in order for one of them to be the first to find a prize; it may be a plastic gnome or perhaps a plastic windmill. Pat and me had to sing our songs perched in the rear of a carriage up by the engine. When we stopped singing it indicated to the guests that the time had come to halt, a sort of 'musical trains,' everyone was happy.

All was well until the end of the journey was in sight, and the ones who had not found a prize realised that the chances of a freebee was diminishing. Some didn't wait for the cue to alight from the train when we stopped singing and leapt from the moving carriages into the undergrowth. They proceeded to steal anything that was not tied down; others on seeing this debacle joined in! Soon the sounds of swearing and breaking plastic could be heard ringing and echoing in the darkness throughout the woods. People emerged from the trees, annoyed at not discovering a prize; some were bloodied by their wrestling a trophy from someone else, whilst some drunkenly carried what they supposed was a prize, but it turned out to be a broken gnome's head, or the sails from a windmill, or even just a bamboo fishing rod, stolen from some unsuspecting gnome! By the time we had made it back to the marquee, the famous and expensive Champagne had begun to be hauled away in crates, and was last seen being loaded into the back of the posh cars. The buggers pinched the lot! We were too busy working to fully enjoy the evening by joining in, but it taught us a lesson in life - not all people with money are nice people! We laughed about this incident for years after, because unbeknown to the guests, whilst we were supposed to entertain them, they were providing entertainment for us! It's a funny old world when you think about it isn't it?

As the years passed, I eventually moved into the commercial world, and Pat and I drifted apart musically, although we did eventually meet up again, soon you will find out how.

Unfortunately, several years after our reunion Pat fell ill. He died a few years ago whilst awaiting a liver transplant

I really miss Pat. He was the best singer I ever worked with. His vocal range was amazing and possibly unique.

GNOME SONG!

Two local singers are hoping to make their fortune — with the help of Dudley's "little people."

Pete Shakespeare (below) and Pat Hannon, who both work in the Dudley branch of Tandy, are shortly to record the "Legend of the Gnomes," written to mark the opening of Dudley Zoo's "Gnomeland."

The words are by entrepreneur Colin Stone, who thought up the whole gno

(1976) Authors Collection

Pete Shakespear & Pat Hannon

(1975) Authors Collection

170

I continued to build up my folk club gigs and was attracting quite a few followers and receiving good press reports, when I unexpectedly received an offer that I could not refuse. I was appearing at a folk club on the same bill as Gerry Lockran when, after the show, Gerry invited me to tour Europe with him! He had been watching me for a while, and felt that we could put together a show that would complement each other, and prove a success with his audience. He had arranged gigs in Holland, Germany, France and Belgium, with a TV appearance in Denmark, to promote a new album of songs, 'Rally Round the Flag.' To help to keep the costs to a minimum, we would sleep in his newly acquired Volkswagen camper van and eat local simple dishes. There was a hard schedule of dates planned. After spending the night at Gerry's house, we drove to the docks at Dover and boarded the ferry early in the morning, just as a storm was brewing.

Many troubadours were on the boat, making their way to begin European tours. At the time John Renbourn had a leg in plaster. He was travelling with Jacqui McShee to fulfil dates for their own tour of Europe which included several television appearances in Germany. As the storm got worse, the action of the ship rolling and pitching ever more violently, moved the chairs from one side of the boat to the other, along with anything else that was not screwed down or lashed. The sea was rough and the boat was beginning to 'take it green!' Poor

John was sitting in a plastic chair and was sliding around all over the place. He was trying to protect his plastered leg with his crutches, and had it stretched out in front of him looking for all the world like the gun on a tank! Hoping not to knock someone over, he was giggling and attempting to make the best of the situation. Eventually, he found a suitable anchorage, and he and Jacqui clung onto each other to weather out the storm. We sought to grab hold onto anything that was screwed down and immovable, and attempted to cling on for dear life! Gerry and I kept each other talking to take our minds off the rolling and pitching - but one poor man, I am sorry to say, lost total control.

We had observed the poor bugger as his face slowly lost its colour. He was trying to keep his eyes focused through the windows and out to the pitching horizon. For some unexplained reason, we had noticed his predicament, and couldn't take our eyes off him. His face eventually turned a shade of green! He began to retch slightly, then looked around sheepishly to see if anyone had seen him. We looked away quickly. We began to giggle, Gerry was a good giggler. The man then reached into his pocket and began to vomit into his handkerchief whilst still trying to maintain his dignity, have you ever tried it? It's nigh on impossible! We held our laughter in, but our eyes began to stream with tears as we watched fascinated. As the movement of the boat got more and more exaggerated, he reached into his luggage to seek out more hankies and promptly filled them with his breakfast, he then threw the items to the deck, creating a ring of slithery mess around him! Things went from bad to worse, as by now he was filling used underpants, towels and shirts, anything to contain the flood emanating from within him. Gerry and I watched in amazement as he was, by now, ashen faced and his red bulging eyes were streaming with tears. He then projectile vomited all over the floor, eventually filling his suitcase! Our sides were bursting, we simply couldn't help it; I suppose we were just as nervous of heaving, so we covered it over with humour, albeit at the expense of another human being. The amazing thing was, as the boat docked in Calais, the man put everything back into his suitcase, closed it, and walked down the gangplank as if nothing had happened! This story kept me and Gerry amused for years. We had never seen anything like it!

We travelled up the Dutch coast to our first engagement, on the way passing massive concrete gun emplacements left over from the war. In Amsterdam, we knew that this tour was going to be a tough one. In the club where we were booked to appear, we opened the show together at around 8.30, playing till about 9.30pm. After a break of about an hour, we continued performing songs alternately, or occasionally one would play backing guitar for the other. Some nights we performed until we dropped, or till the last customers left in the early hours.

We lived in Gerry's camper van and after several days we were feeling a bit rough. Thankfully, however, we managed to shower at a fan's house before moving on. Before a concert in Enschede in Holland, we decided to get our hair washed at the local barbers. What a performance it was trying to explain to a very polite old Dutch barber that all we wanted was a hair vashen!! und dryen. The waiting customers were poking each other in the ribs and giggling at us silly hairy Englishmen, but we eventually emerged with suitably coiffured hair, and were now feeling good before the show.

We found accommodation in the house of a Dutch couple who had helped to organise some of the bookings in Holland. Even here we played until the early hours entertaining the family. During the morning, Helen, the young lady who we were staying with, took us to shop in the nearby town. In the market place in Oldenzaal was a cheese stall where she stopped to buy the ingredients to make lunch. The large, red cheeked, Dutch stallholder beckoned me over and gave me a wedge of cheese to eat. Politely, I said no thank you - it was like a big slice of cake! He spoke with my companion quite earnestly, and then she turned to me and said that I must eat it. She related that as a child, the man's village had been liberated by British troops at the end of the war, and he was forever grateful. It was a gesture of goodwill that he wanted to share his food with me; you never think that history could become so real - a touching moment for all of us.

I can't remember all the dates, but the tour was long and arduous; some of the dates were: Oldenzaal, Enschede, Sella, Aachen, Munster, Frankfurt, Cologne, Osnabruck and Copenhagen. We dined daily on pieces of German bread, Edam cheese and fresh jam, with of course, a bottle of beer! As we travelled along we would swap stories and sing songs. Kris Kristofferson's, 'Me and Bobby McGee' was a favourite. It reminded Gerry of how he was missing his wife Bobby and the boys. We used to discuss for hours the meaning of life and why we are here, but Gerry was captivated by an experience he had had whilst a student in India.

Gerry was the son of an Irish engineer and an Indian mother and had been sent to a boarding school, somewhere in India, I don't recall where, but obviously he was being absorbed into that culture. Gerry told me that the Indian people have many Gods, but one deity in particular is a golden lady that flies through the sky. The distinguishing feature of this God is that she apparently had her feet turned backwards and had little wings on her ankles. Gerry reverently related the story about how one afternoon there was a big commotion at the school and all the kids rushed to one side of the building to see this God flying past! - With great excitement, Gerry declared,

'I saw her with my own eyes man, I swear!'

He used to tell of the Indian Holy men who regularly

travelled from village to village curing the sick! He told a story about the time a Holy man came to his village, and a lady with cancer approached him, and requested to be healed. A crowd of villagers surrounded the scene, with Gerry and the other kids looking on. After much chanting, raising of hands and praying, she was declared to be healed! To quote our dear Gerry, 'The cancer dropped out of her arse man, I saw it!' (If anyone knew Gerry and can recall his gravelly voice you can hear him saying it can't you.) We used to frighten the lives out of ourselves, telling ghost stories and regaling other daft tales, but for the most part we laughed and played our music like two happy puppies let on the loose. How I miss him!

The van became our home, until we got to a place called Nottuln in Germany, where we stayed with the concert promoter and record executive of Autogramme records. He was promoting the annual Folk and Blues Festival at Osnabruck. After listening to me rehearse, he felt that my music was a bit too commercial and decided not to sign me, but he said he would use me in the concerts. Little did we both realise then just what was in store. The concert here was to become a highlight of the tour for me. I am so glad that I kept the poster and programme for old times' sake. A lot of the great people who were on the bill are sadly no longer with us.

Authors Collection

```
   P r o g r a m m f o l g e        Fertig ausprogrammiert ist das FOLK MEKKA in der
                                     Fachhochschule, Albrechtstr. am besten zu erreich
   es ist möglich, daß sich         über die Lotter-Str./Bundesstr.55, dann in die
   die Folge verschiebt, die        spitze Gabelung / Lieneschweg fahren,denn die 2.
   Ansage hat PETER BOLL.           Straße rechts = Caprivistraße, wobei die Verlänger-
                                     ung die Albrechtstr.ist, dort ist die FH unüber-
   FOLK- MEKKA:                      sehbar/ neue Architektur-'Betonfestung'.

I Konzert, 14 Uhr Aula der FH:
1) GERRY LOCKRAN (London)      Solist    Im Gr.Saal des Hauses der Jugend werden
2) TAIL TOODLE (Holland)       Quartett  folgende Künstler in langen Sets während
                                         der genannten Konzerte vorgestellt:
3) JO-ANN KELLY              Solistin &
   PETER EMERY  (London)       Duo       1.Hauptkonzert am Freitag, 20 Uhr:
4) THE ORIGINAL BUSHWHACKERS &           IAIN MACKINTOSH         Die Ansage am Freitag
   BULLOCKIES BUSH BAND                  LES FRERES PENNEC       und Sonntag besorgt
   (Australien)                Quintett  MAUREEN & JOHN PAPE     Peter Boll.
                                         GERRY LOCKRAN
5) KEITH PEARSON & PAUL CRAS-            THE BUSHWHACKERS
   WELL (Irland/England)       Duo
                                         2.Hauptkonzert am Samstag 14 Uhr:
6) RICHARD BARGEL (Köln)       Solist
                                         KEELROW                 Die Ansage am Samstag
7) CHARLIE & THEODOR (Essen)   Duo       DETLEV KÖHLER           im Haus der Jugend hat
                                         FIEDEL MICHEL           JIM DEERY (Irland)
8) DOUG PORTER (England)       Solist    PETER BELLAMY
                                         BUKKA WHITE?
9) FROGMORTON (England)        Sextett
                                         3.Hauptkonzert am Samstag 20 Uhr:
II Konzert, 20 Uhr Aula der FH:          CHARLIE & THEODOR       Für alle Konzerte:
                                         RICHARD BARGEL          Herumlaufen nur in den
10) THE SANDS (Nordirland)     Quartett  DOUG PORTER             Umbaupausen (Künstler-
11) LES FRERES PENNEC (Bretagne) Duo     PETE SHAKESPEARE (London)   wechsel)
12) PETER BELLAMY (England)    Solist    FROGMORTON
13) PARALIPOMENA (Dinklage)    Duo       Studiokonzert am Sonntag 13 Uhr Kl.Saal
14) DETLEV KÖHLER (Recklinghausen) Solist u.a. BEPPO (Osnabrück)
15) FIEDEL MICHEL (Münster)    Trio
16) JOHN & MAUREEN PAPE (England) Duo    4.Hauptkonzert am Sonntag 15 Uhr:
17) BUKKA WHITE ? (USA)        Solist    TAIL TOODLE
                                         KEITH PEARSON & PAUL CRASWELL
18) KEELROW (England)          Sextett   THE SANDS FAMILY
19) IAIN MACKINTOSH (Schottland) Solist  & in session with IAIN MACKINTOSH
20) THE SANDS FAMILY (wie 10)  Quartett
21) SESSION aus 19/20).        - Schluß - 5.Hauptkonzert am Sonntag 19.30 Uhr:
                                         PARALIPOMENA
Hinweis: Falls die Zeit noch reicht,     JO ANN KELLY      außerdem die an anderer
evtl.v.Bukka White,oder es dem Publikum und  PETE EMERY    Stelle geschilderte FOLK-
dem Hausmeister-Personal zumutbar ist, das   DR.ROSS       einführung mit vergleichen-
Abendprogramm bis weit nach Mitternacht zu   PAPE (gr.öff. den Beispielen und Gesprächs
überziehen, werden laut Ansage ggf.zusätz-   Workshop)     einblende mit den PAPES
liche Künstler bzw.Programmpunkte eingefügt.               (wahrsch.nach einer Pause
                                                           ca.22.15 Uhr,in der diaje-
IN DER AULA ist R a u c h v e r b o t !!!                  nigen Besucher des Festival
(bitte auch keine Flaschen mit reinnehmen...)             verlassen können,die die
                                                           letzten Züge/Busse/Autos usw
                                                           erreichen müssen).
- - - - - - - - - - - - - - - - - - - - - - - - - - - - - - - - - - - - - - - - - -
Den Dauerkarten-Inhabern ist es erlaubt, mit ihrer Karte auch die Aula der FH zu be-
suchen. Im Haus der Jugend wird natürlich ein weiteres Komplementär-Programm geboten,
welches der Ansage zu entnehmen ist. Manche engl.Namen werden nicht immer verstanden,
deshalb hier schriftlich: RICK BOWERS (USA), GILDEROY (engl.Trio), JOHN STEELE (Engl.)
EAMON (Schottl.), LYNN & KARIN (Engl.), CHALKIE WHITE, DAVE & DILL, ANGUS & JIM (alle
Großbritannien), wahrsch.auch GREG BYRNE (Engländer), MICHAEL HUGHES (Belfast) beide i
                                                                         Deutschl.lebend.
```

Authors Collection

At this concert the camaraderie between the entertainers was the best I ever came across.

Sometimes, there could be a bit of pettiness among some in the folk world as to who would be better received by the audience, and who was the bigger star; because of this I tended to limit myself to a small circle of friends - so to experience the atmosphere at the festival was for me very refreshing. The acts were taken from the best of British, European and American Folk and Blues. The top of the bill was to be B.B. King's cousin, Bukka White, an old true blues legend.

I remember Gerry and me visiting the local youth house, where the gymnasium had been turned into a teaching workshop for the festival. We listened to several workshops on different aspects of Folk from all over Europe, but notably we enjoyed John and Maureen Pape expounding the intricacies of the banjo. When they recognised us, they sent a bottle of Cointreau spinning across the floor for us to enjoy, great artistes and wonderful people, a truly lovely atmosphere. A young German lad stopped us to talk. Although he had partaken of a few steins of ale, he spoke good English, albeit with a New York accent, which we thought was a bit odd. When Gerry asked him where he had learned to speak English, he replied, 'From gramophone records!' It's a strange world isn't it? The trouble was that the boy sounded like Kermit the frog! Once again we had another giggling session!

I had been staying in a small hotel in Osnabruck for the duration of the festival, when unexpectedly, I was notified that

Bukka White had pulled out at the last minute. Suddenly, I found myself being collected from my hotel, ushered into a fast car and sped across the city - to be put on in his place! Travelling to the theatre, my heart was pounding in trepidation - I really didn't know how on earth I was going to pull this one off! Backstage there was an air of panic. No one but the show's promoter, and some people from the audience who had previously seen Gerry and I perform on the tour, had heard me play. I was bundled through the stage door and told to wait in the wings for my cue. I heard the compere introduce me .... 'From London, Pete Shakespear,' and I was pushed out onto the stage. The stage itself seemed a mile long. There was a packed house, three tiers of seated expectant fans, the audience was massive. They obviously weren't there to see me! In the opposite wings was a recording studio, recording the show for a live album and at the same time putting the show out live to millions across the continent. In the spotlight, the banks of microphones were arranged as if they were expecting a presidential address. I wanted to run away and vomit! I summoned all my confidence, and, as I spoke the words, 'Hello good evening,' ...... the mikes all went silent ....., shit, the P.A. had fused! I anxiously looked to the wings for help - a few moments later, with thumbs up from the engineer, we were off into the first number.

After I finished the song, a great cheer went up from the

crowd; I had got 'em! The set went down a storm. As I came off stage, I was mobbed by a crowd, whose words for the most part I could not understand due to the different languages, and there was a phalanx of cameras and reporters who were seeking a picture and a story. I was shaking like a leaf from the exertion, then Gerry appeared through the crowd to congratulate me and give me a big slap on the back. I had pulled it out of the bag - but I don't know how! It was a delight meeting people from all over the world.

When the German festival was over, Gerry had to go on to Denmark to complete a booking, and I had to get back to the U.K. to fulfil pre arranged concerts. However, Gerry had kindly arranged a lift for me to take me back home to England.

I have to say that Gerry Lockran was the most generous person in show business that I have ever met. His kindness and lack of 'big-star-itis' was unforgettable. He was so talented and original that he had no fear of sharing his experiences and expertise with other musicians who he felt to be genuine. It was, indeed, the greatest privilege to have known Gerry. It's really sad that this business takes so many talented people. Perhaps it is the lifestyle, the booze, or for some, the drugs, but I believe it's because the really great ones are feeling, sensitive souls, who give their all to entertain, and it can burn the emotions up and break bodies and minds very quickly.

Scene Three

<u>On my way to Stay</u>

(1974) Authors Collection

Gerry had arranged for me to hitch a lift back to the UK with a band called 'The Sands Family,' truly great songwriters and musicians.

The band were all members of the same family hailing from County Down in Ireland, Tommy, Colm, Eugene and Anne, playing traditional instruments, making beautiful sounds. They had completed a series of engagements in Europe which had earned them a hit record in Berlin called 'All The Little Children,' and culminated with the appearance at the festival in Osnabruck. Very kindly, they allowed me to busk along at a couple of their gigs, perhaps recognising the bond that all true musicians have, if they have spent any time at all 'on the road.'

As we wearily made our way to the coast, somewhere, on the autobahn in Belgium, the van broke down. A couple of the lads slid down the embankment on to the road below and found an Esso service station, just under a bridge outside a little town I had never heard of .... I don't know where it was even to this day. The little garage was run by a Belgian man and his wife; he being the mechanic and she looking after the sales kiosk. In broken English the man said he would tow the van back to his garage. After a brief examination of our sad transport, he informed us that the alternator had packed up; he could repair it, but couldn't get the parts until the next morning. This left us with time to kill, but thankfully, this man and his wife, turned out to be really lovely, kind, hospitable human beings. We shared our cheese and wine, music and stories. The couple even gave up their bed for Ann, whilst we lads slept in the van which was parked overnight in the workshop. The next day, after the van had been repaired, the band decided to set up on the forecourt of the garage to perform a 'Thank you' concert. - The small town was brought to a complete standstill. It was a real joy to see these lovely Belgian people dancing to the Irish gigs and reels produced by these wonderful musicians. This is one of my fondest memories.

It proved to be far more difficult getting back into the U.K. than leaving it, and brought us down to earth with an almighty bump. We were stopped by customs at Europort and made to strip out all the equipment and have our baggage searched. We wondered what on earth they were looking for. Obviously they found nothing and waved us through. We were stopped again, just a short distance further on, and were made to repeat the whole process! The officers were getting more and more short tempered. Once more, nothing was found, and we hurriedly re-loaded the van. By this time, boarding time for the ferry home was fast approaching and tempers were getting short. We were waved off, ... and then, yet again, after another few yards, we were stopped! By now, we too were getting hot under the collar. This time they virtually stripped the van of every panel and almost every nut and bolt. Nothing was found, and finally they reluctantly let us through in order to board a boat for home. What on earth was the matter with them we never knew; I guess it was our appearance that brought us to their attention, hairy and a bit scruffy, combined with the fact that 'The Sands' had Irish accents. We were all totally blameless, and very tired indeed by the time we boarded and finally got back to the U.K.

Some years later, I saw another Sands family member advertised at a folk club, and for old times' sake decided to drop in for a listen. I didn't know that there was a younger member of this family, Ben Sands, and he also typically exuded the soft Irish charm of the story teller. He said that at the time we were touring he was too young to be on the road. Now, Ben carries on the great tradition of travelling folkies, entertaining all over the world, a wonderfully talented man.

On returning back to the U.K., I continued plying my songs around the Folk circuit.

At a club one evening, I was approached by Jon Tame, a bass guitar player, who thought it would be a good idea to get a folk band together, made up of old friends who he had performed with in the past. In my previous life, as you have seen, I was used to stage companions around me, so I was interested in what Jon had to offer.

It can be a lonely old life as a solo performer, but at least you don't get the problems with spouses and other musician's girlfriends, who were mostly jealous of their men, or each other, and who were afraid to let the men out of their sight.

In one band I was with, a couple of the girlfriends missed their men so much that they began to sleep together - eventually becoming lovers. The boyfriends discovered them, by accident, in bed together. Oops, they gave them a good beating and summarily kicked them out of the house!

I played a couple of gigs with a band that had a lead guitarist whose wife, as we left his house for the show, would literally slap his face red and tell him in no uncertain terms what would happen if he ever strayed. He never answered her back, or raised his hand; he said that she only acted like that when she was on a period. I felt so sorry for him, but it was his marriage, and after about two shows I couldn't stand the friction anymore and called it a day, poor bastard!

It is understandable to be wary I suppose, but if you date a musician you had better know what you are letting yourself in for. It's not always the fault of the men. During my time in the night club scene I can honestly say that the women were more predatory. Some ladies, after a few drinks, would get up to the most strange things, and offer or attempt the most outrageous activities, especially if they thought you were, or were about to become, rich and famous. One young lady, I recall, would be found naked in the back of the van before any of the gear could be loaded. How on earth she got in, I don't know. I have also known of four and five piece bands, all contracting something nasty, at the same time off the same lady! It's disconcerting to think that these voluptuous souls would be old ladies now, but remember, I know what grandma did!!

It was in this atmosphere of mutual mistrust, that we

experienced a lot of resistance to forming a new band from the wives and girlfriends of the musicians who Jon was attempting to attract. Obviously, they had moved on and their lives had changed, most were now married with families and mortgages. We had, therefore, decided to make it a duo after all, when Ken Price, (a wonderful acoustic guitarist from a well respected folk band called 'Marie Celeste,' that he and Jon had played for previously) decided he would join us. I am really glad that he did, because his acoustic guitar playing was second to none; as can be heard expressed so beautifully on the track, 'Once more,' from the album 'Stay.' We performed well together, and were delighted to receive an invitation to record an album of songs for a small label called Real Records, (RR2001), part of the Folk Heritage stable. The title track chosen for the album was 'Stay,' the song that had impressed EMI, A&R man Norman Smith. It was shortly after the album was released, that Ken decided to quit the trio, and get married. We were back to a duo. It was also about this time that I met the love of my life, Penny, (she told me to say this!! but more later.)

I came across a press cutting from the Wolverhampton Chronicle of 1974, which said in part that, 'Pete Shakespear has forsaken the pop scene for the freedom of folk clubs,' ..... well that was not strictly true was it?

The album was recorded in 1975, in a studio at Montgomery, Wales. The whole thing was put together in a day, hence many of the rough edges, but the idea was that we send it out as an advertising tool to try and obtain more bookings. The sleeve notes were written by Jon Betmead, resident of a great folk club, held at 'The Olde Bull Inne,' in Royston, Hertfordshire. Jon performed many a time in bare feet; he had a great personality and was a wonderful entertainer. I remember the time when he held the crowd at Cambridge in the palm of his hand, ... wonderful! Jon Tame and I enjoyed many super nights in the folk clubs. It is nice to know that people still have a fondness for the songs on the album, particularly 'Stay' and 'Once More.'

I think we still hold the record for the biggest audience at 'The Butts Tavern' in Walsall, which was then run by Andy Caven, who himself toured for many years with a singer called Rosie Hardman.

Sometimes, during my portrayal of a song, I have been known to get a bit carried away. The poor old Epiphone guitar received a beating one night when I got a bit excited, thumping out the rhythm to Dobie Gray's 'Drift Away,' and I put my fist through the old girl! It must have been becoming a habit of mine. I remember the first time I went on a folk club stage; it was just a few planks, supported on some orange boxes. Feeling the beat and getting really in the groove, so to speak, and stamping out a rhythm to a blues called, 'I Aint Gonna Be Treated This Way,' I promptly put my sandaled foot through the stage!

Occasionally, I meet old folkies who say to me, 'Hey, Shakey, remember when .....' and proceed to tell a tale of something I did that I have absolutely no recollection of! I popped into a folk club recently to see a blues player who has been around for a while. On seeing me and my family enter the room, he exclaimed, 'I see Pete Shakespear is in the audience, I remember once when him and me downed a couple of bottles of whisky one night in the 1970's, Oh what a night that was!' Truth to tell, I never supped with the man. There are quite a few 'urban myths' still flying around, I was never that bad, surely?

I was going to call this book by an expression, 'The best of order,' which was used by a wonderful compere and host who ran a lovely club in Heath Hayes near Cannock in Staffordshire. He was a softly spoken Irishman named Laurie Ward, and he always introduced the guests with: 'The very best of order, will you welcome our guests for the evening ...... '

I still think that Laurie's delivery of this unique introduction inspired good manners from the audience, and respect from the performers. That's one thing I will always remember from that club, and the folk clubs in general - good manners. His wife Jean had a truly lovely voice and was usually accompanied by Terry McCann on piano. Jean's interpretation of, 'Till The White Rose Blooms Again,' would make ones hair stand on end, beautiful.

We always tried to make it through to the gig whatever the weather and not let people down. Once, on a really foggy night, we got ourselves lost in the Black Country, we could not see more than a couple of yards in front of the car. My girlfriend Penny, who was by now travelling everywhere with me, decided to walk in front of the car to read the street signs. We finally made it to the club, and were so pleased to see an audience waiting for us. I think the club was called 'The Saltwells.'

I used to enjoy a club in St Ives, Cornwall - 'Mr Peggotty's.' Here, as you entered the club door, you collected a bean bag from a large pile in the corner, a wine bottle with a candle in the top, and then sought out a quiet spot for yourself to enjoy the evening's singers. There was also a nice atmosphere at a place called 'The Smugglers,' in St Erth; the holiday makers just wanted to be entertained with a good sing song!

I performed at 'The Penbeagle Croft' in St Ives one night, by accident. It happened this way ......

I had arranged to take a break with a couple of likely lads, who I had met whilst spending the summer working temporarily at a large factory, when bookings were slow. They fancied a camping holiday, so I borrowed a tent from an old pal and agreed to meet them at the station early one Saturday morning. We caught the train West. It was all going well; the banter was good and we were getting along famously, although

I did notice that they were consuming large volumes of the amber liquid. By the end of the second day of the 'holiday,' they had drunk, and given to the local bookies, most of their spending money. We retired from the beach to spend the evening at 'The Penbeagle Croft,' and enjoy a couple of pints and a pasty, before making our way back up the hill to the farm where we were camped. Some people never learn do they? The ale started talking!! One of the fools had had too much to drink and was getting a bit truculent. With a downward chopping action, he was explaining to me how he, 'had been trained to kill using his bare hands' when he had been a member of the S.A.S. - I don't think he twigged that I was a giggler! He turned a bit nasty when I said that I didn't believe him, and he began to cast doubt on both my parentage and my ability to entertain. The fool of a man beckoned over the landlord.

'Landlord, go and fetch your old guitar, my pal here reckons he can play!'

Thrust into my hands was a guitar which had not been played for so long that the strings were green! I embarrassingly said that I wouldn't play as I had no way to put the beast into concert pitch.

'Oh no, mate, you play!' - slobbered the arsehole.

By now, I was embarrassed and angry, and with nowhere to go and no way out, I quietly hummed a tune that I knew off by heart, and tried my utmost to put the guitar into the best pitch I could and attempt to tune the monster. When I felt it was about right, I let rip! I had a wonderful night! The pub was full of holiday makers, primarily Geordies. What great people. A big bloke went round and filled several pint glasses with money. That shut our matey up, especially when I refused to buy his beer! That night, on returning to the campsite, I made plans to return to the Midlands. The next day, amidst a barrage of anger and threats, I took down the tent, walked to the station and left them to sort themselves out.

After a couple of weeks, on returning to the factory, I approached the loudmouth's brother who also worked there, and told him what had happened. I explained that, because of the incident in St Ives, his brother would probably not be speaking to me.

'Don't worry,' he said,

'He always gets like that when he is pissed, and he was in the catering corps for three years not the S.A.S. the silly bugger!' To cap it all, I later learned that because they had no money and nowhere to sleep, the two fools had to rough it on the harbour wall, (then known as the 'hippies wall,' due to the number of 'hairies' sleeping under the stars and partying there). They were unfortunately robbed of their possessions, including the frying pan I'd left them with, ah well! So much for killer hands!

Over the years, I grew very fond of St Ives; wonderful days, bare feet, sun and pasties, you can't beat it! We lived in the South West for some years and I still enjoy visiting whenever I can, although sad to say, the old place has changed.

Long gone are the quiet streets, the cats, the men in flat caps mending fishing nets on the harbour wall. The copper ships lanterns and dimly lit pubs. The sounds of clinking beer glasses and fishermen's banter emanating from the Sloop Inn. Today, the old town appears to be infected with modern cafes, shiny aluminium chairs and glass facades. The homes, once lived in by fishermen and their families, are now holiday apartments or second homes for posh people, and it seems there is nowhere to park anymore. When I do go back, I find myself remembering .... the girl in the newsagents, the old lady in the stores on the back road, the old couple who used to sit outside the 'Dolls House,' they always had time to chat. The maroon sounding across the darkened town on a stormy night. The clamour of running feet as the brave men rushed from their beds to crew the lifeboat. The tractor used to trundle it through the street to be launched from the beach, perhaps into a raging sea or maybe just for an evening's rescue drill. Artists quietly painting the harbour and it's little working boats, and a clay potter skilfully making it look easy to throw a jug or a vase. It's so different from the pictures and mass produced ornaments now imported from foreign lands and displayed in the windows of once owned local shops and family businesses. The light is still beautiful and enchanting .... but the peace we used to enjoy seems to have gone. It's probably me, but I don't like change that much.

I once attended an audition to join a troupe for a summer season in Jersey. We took ourselves along to the workingmen's club where the audition was being held, accompanied by a heavily pregnant friend of ours who ran a club in Halesowen in Worcestershire, Barbara Johnson. She came along for the ride and had not completed an entry form to take part. I did a couple of songs, but the chap organising it didn't seem impressed. I don't think I would have fitted in. The show they were trying to get together was for a season playing in a hotel to pensioners. The troupe were working on several sketches with costume changes, some even involving wigs and drag. The show was to include a number complete with bagpipes and kilt! Realising that the act was not for me, and feeling more than a little theatrical, Barbara asked the organiser if she could have a go. Reluctantly, he agreed, and she took to the stage; standing there looking for all the world like a waif and stray. You could hear a pin drop as, with one hand on her baby bump, she sang 'Liverpool Lullaby.' Little ooh's and aah's were heard from the audience, several old ladies wiped a tear away with their handkerchief. When she finished singing, she brought the house down, and was promptly offered the gig!

There is nothing more enjoyable to me than to hear people having a good laugh, but when I was enjoying myself at a club one evening .... I relaxed a bit too much!

I began to tell a story that was best kept as a musicians' joke and was really rude. I saw Penny sitting in the front row of the audience, her face turning ashen, and she motioned to me, 'You can't tell that joke,' 'Why?' I said, in my euphoric state, 'You can't tell it, just think of the ending.' .... Oh my goodness!!!

The audience by now were up for it and curious as to the ending. I was having kittens; this joke really should never have been heard outside certain circles. I said to the audience that perhaps I had gone too far and that I had suddenly become aware how filthy the joke was, and can I stop please ....?!

From the crowd came the chant, 'Finish it, finish it!'

Not for the first time in my musical history, once again I had nowhere to run, I had to go on, and eventually, embarrassingly I reached the punch line. The audience gasped and sat there open mouthed. Penny sank down lower in her seat, praying for the ground to open up and swallow her, oh dear, I did it again!! A lesson that there should be no such thing as an ad lib! Engage brain before opening mouth! Incidentally, we have to thank dear Gerry for this one, we used to giggle about it every time we met, the punch line was 'The Debonairs,' .... but it's not what you think! and anyway I suspect he got it from Brimstone, because old Derek loved a laugh.

We have performed with a few strange ones over the years. I remember a disastrous booking with Jake Thackray. I think he was becoming disillusioned with performing. He kept himself to himself and had that look in his eyes as though he might take an axe to you at any minute! The show turned belly up when the promoter wouldn't pay us the agreed fee! But, I have to say that this was the only occasion it ever happened to me, in all my time playing the folk clubs. The agreed terms for the gig were usually sealed with a handshake. Most folk clubs were run by true ladies and gentlemen, and honourable people; this particular one wasn't, and we never worked for him again.

Perhaps it's best that this part of the story doesn't come over as a who's who of the folk days, because I have no doubt we all had our favourites. However, I thought it might be nice to mention several of the acts who were pretty decent people, and I'm sure that you too, if you had the chance to see them perform, found them as entertaining as I did.

A few funny men made us laugh. The late, great, Tony Capstick was funny on and off stage. I loved to hear him sing 'Mr Punch and Judy Man,' and his rendition of the Hovis wholemeal bread commercial will live on forever.

I nearly died of laughing one night, listening to Bernard Wrigley, performing a routine about the pool collector's plums getting stuck in the wardrobe door. What a great talent; his character of Dodgy Eric in Peter 'Kay's Phoenix Nights' perfectly illustrated the natural humour he possesses.

The Brownsville's put on a good show too, their big

bumble bee in the audience was brilliantly funny, as was their routine, 'I'm In The Mood For Love.'

I still regularly play an album by Jack Hudson, and of course, old Lockran, especially when I get a bit sentimental, and I think that performers like Keb Mo and Eric Bibb are terrific examples of the modern day troubadour.

It's strange though, that one now famous funny man, who will remain nameless, ... but who became very popular on British television, even having his own series, ... was one of the most miserable buggers off stage I have ever met! He would never mix with the other acts, being happy to content himself with his own company. He could often be seen perched on a bar stool, well away from the rest, sipping half a bitter shandy. If he could work it in to his act, he would include a bit of piss taking out of the others taking part in the show; I don't know why he performed at folk clubs, but the alternative comedy scene hadn't yet got underway, and I suppose there were few avenues at that time for his type of humour.

Someone once asked me about traditional folk music, ... well, certain performers didn't like the idea that our music was commercial, and some clubs would not tolerate such impurity being expressed in their sensitive ears! There are, however, some traditional tunes that I do still enjoy. One song, when done properly, was 'The Shearing's Not For You,' and of course, 'Go Lassie Go,' (perhaps the folk world's national anthem) -

wonderful, and the 'Ripley Wayfarers' singing just about anything, but in particular, 'Bread and Fishes.' But personally, I find it difficult to understand, when perhaps three or four big hairy men and a girl get up to sing, whereupon they all appear to stare down at the stage floor. Into the mystic they go, with one hand in their pocket or holding a pint of beer, and with the forefinger of the other hand in their ear! Hey ho, each to his own! .... and what on earth is Morris dancing all about?! Most of these folk were likely teachers and academics who enjoyed the history and customs of old English folk music. Like I said, each to his own, harmless enough .... but not for me. Most of the crowd I knew, steered clear of a 'Traddy' club, but if for some reason, you hadn't done your research and inadvertently found that you had a booking at such a venue, then I am afraid you went down like a lead balloon and the atmosphere could be a bit fraught!

Some folk always wanted the last spot, as if it were the top of the bill, oh dear! If you are good enough, you don't have to be placed top of the bill, the audience will do that for you! Yes, there was many a long face when you got a better reception from the audience than ones who thought that they were long established and favoured. But I have no time for petty jealousies. The real pros who I have worked with were not that way. The Four Tops were not jealous of Jimmy James and the Vagabonds, or Gerry Lockran of Long John Baldry, not at all.

We are all different and there is room for everybody if you have the talent. A favourite saying of mine is:

'A candle loses none of its own light when it lights another;'

....think about it!

Occasionally, between engagements in order to relax, Biffo Griffiths and I would take ourselves out into the country to a little pub which was used in a television advertisement for Ansell's beer, 'The New Inns' at Kiddemore Green, near Brewood, Staffordshire. The landlord's name was Archibald Bent. We called the place Archie's for obvious reasons - I still do, but the old place has changed out of all recognition since Archie and Helen his wife passed away. Over the years a series of 'townies' have tried to make a go of it, taking down walls, putting in a juke box and keg beer; one even taking it on as a hobby pub. Then it was closed most of the time, only opening up when he felt in the mood! Various managers have put tarmac over the rose garden and taken out the log fires, totally ruining what they saw in the business in the first place. Archie was an ex-RAF type, with cravat and accent to match. He and Helen were great hosts. Helen loved her cruises on the old Queen Mary and she would talk for hours about her trips. Every time Biffo and I appeared through the door, Archie would say, in a typical military voice, 'Hello you ragged arse beggars, and where have you two heathens been? What are you going to have to drink?' Only Archie could get away with it. With a broad smile he would quickly produce our favourite poison at the time, Pernod and lemonade.

One evening, a man who was on holiday at a camping and caravan site not far from the Inn, walked into the off licence part of 'Archie's' - remember them? As Archie slid up the little window of the off licence to serve him, the man recognised Biffo standing at the bar. Biffo said,

'Have a drink,' and beckoned him to join us,

'No thanks mate,' he said, 'I've got the wife and kids in the caravan and I only popped out for some crisps and pop.'

'Oh, go on,' Biffo insisted, 'have a swift half.'

'Well alright then,' he replied.

We began relating our latest adventures to Archie and his wife, with Biffo's guest listening intently. He left Archie's way after eleven o'clock, very well oiled and giggling, I wonder if his wife ever forgave him!

Once, Biffo, in a vain attempt to be helpful, talked a very naive landlord into letting me play the piano, in exchange for money collected in a pint mug and 'a few beers,' for his friends. Well, to say that Biff and his cronies can put it away is probably an understatement. The evening's entertainment began very amicably. I ran through a couple of Ray Charles' standards, the landlord smiled, the little crowd of older regulars clapped. After a while I took a short break and had a pint. On returning to the piano stool, I discovered that I had suddenly developed a partnership with another so called pianist! Biffo, by now was well inebriated, and he wanted things to be more up tempo. He started to attempt to play the piano, only to create an almighty racket as he had no idea where his fingers were, let alone which keys he should be playing!

I rattled through 'The Letter,' the Joe Cocker version, and was just about to move into 'Honky Tonk Woman,' when Biffo suddenly disappeared! He had fallen off the stool! The landlord, breathing fire and sulphur, enquired where the rest of them were. I said that I didn't know, but the landlord could sniff out trouble like an old bloodhound and discovered them all collapsed behind the bar! While everyone's attention had been diverted by my performing antics, the beggars had crept behind the bar and quaffed as much beer as they could in the shortest time available and rendered themselves unconscious. He threw the reprobates into the street, apologising to me and giving me advice to choose my friends more wisely next time!

We had a good friend at the Rock Hotel in Tettenhall, Wolverhampton, where there was a small folk club. Barry Roberts ran the establishment, and some Saturday evenings, after all the guests had gone to bed and the bar emptied, he would arrange a little concert in a back room for his chosen companions, including members of the Wolverhampton School of Music and any visiting artistes to the local theatre, such as Sadler's Wells. One such regular guest was Peter Snape. Peter had been a tailor, and although now long retired, he was always immaculately dressed. He would arrive and take a seat at the bar at about eleven in the evening and remain there till sometime in the early hours of the morning. His favourite tipple was pink gin. He would leave as immaculately turned out as when he arrived - and not a wobble to be seen, a true gentleman. Peter made the clothes for Sir Norman Wisdom, in the early days; the little jacket and cap were his pride and joy. He was delighted to receive a card each Christmas from his old friend in the Isle of Man.

Occasionally, a couple of members of the staff would dress up and perform a ballet to recorded music. The silver service waiter, also named Barry, would be distinguished from Barry the boss by being called 'Little Barry.' He would don a tutu and silk tights and take on the role of Dame Margot Fonteyn, whilst Jenny the receptionist would become Rudolph Nureyev. To say that the sketch was funny is an understatement. Together they floated around the room, often falling over themselves with laughter. 'Little Barry' though, was discovered to have a problem. The scotch whisky levels in the optics behind the bar, would, over the course of an evening, slowly go down, and little Barry would become more and more animated. Barry the boss had clocked this. When little Barry was asked to explain himself, he became a bit truculent, and the last we saw of him that night was when Barry Roberts flung him out of the double doors and into the car park, - followed closely by his shoes!

He was seen back at his job several days later looking suitably chastised, and promising never to do it again!

I called in to the hotel one Saturday evening. Barry Roberts seemed pre-occupied and was unresponsive when I spoke to him; I assumed he must be rushed off his feet, so I abandoned the idea that we would be partying later that night, and moved on somewhere else. Sadly, the following Monday morning, Barry Roberts was found dead. Due to a family misunderstanding that had grown out of all proportion, he had taken his own life. There is an old saying isn't there: 'The graveyards are full of men who thought they understood women.' I don't think that any of the gang realised there was a problem, or we would have encouraged him to talk about it. As it was, Barry was a proud man, a silent type, who kept his feelings to himself. When Bryan rang with the shocking news, my legs buckled under me, how very, very sad!

On a more cheery note, a memorable highlight I recall with pride, was when 'Shakespear' performed at the 10th Anniversary Cambridge Folk Festival, held in the grounds of Cherry Hinton Hall. Established around 1965, the Festival became well known for its eclectic mix of what might be termed folk music. It was renowned for its friendly atmosphere and became the annual mecca for folkies. I recall the organiser, Alex Atterson, having kittens trying to accommodate all those wanting to play a couple of songs in the club tent. Festivals have now become 'the thing,' but there weren't many back then, so it was an opportunity for folkies to gather together and immerse themselves in the great music of the time.

For Jon Tame, one time organiser of Brewood folk club, Saturday is rather special. Jon goes back to the club as a fully-fledged guest singer. Jon has had a chequered career as a folk singer, but seems to have broken through after teaming up with another local singer, Pete Shakespeare. The duo, pictured above, have made quite an impact in local clubs, and also won much acclaim with an appearance at the Cambridge festival.

Folk Diary

Several local folk clubs have closed down for August, but Pete Hancox is keeping his club at the Three Stirrups, Brewood going, and it seems to be thriving. Guests this Saturday are Jon Tame and Pete Shakespeare, and forthcoming dates include: Bill Caddick (Aug 31), Andy Dwyer (Sept 7) and Crumbling Bandwagon (Sept 14).

(1974) Authors Collection

The crowd was something like a massive 10,000. Nowadays, at a big festival, that would be dwarfed, ... but it's still a lot of faces staring back at you.

It is good to be surrounded by such talented people, not only the performers, but also the technicians. I have to confess, I am not very good at understanding the complexities of the mixing desk, I am always glad of their kindness and patience when attempting to balance the dials and knobs - I prefer to leave it to the professionals. We spent many happy hours catching up with old friends and meeting many well known acts from the folk music world, as well as having an opportunity to meet many sincere music fans. Often we played into the night with a tent full of admirers who didn't feel sleepy. The top of the bill, I think, was an Australian band called the Bushwhackers, but Gerry was there, Derek Brimstone, Johnny Silvo, Cliff Aungier, and many others.

Throughout most of the U.K., there was an abundance of really good folk clubs, where the audiences were friendly and loved a good sing song. We grew fond of these people and made friends all over the country. I miss this camaraderie. I well remember the first time I heard a song called 'The Wild Rover,' in a Wolverhampton club. I was amazed as the audience banged their beer glasses on the table during the chorus, whilst singing their hearts out! The respect shown to singers was wonderful, in total contrast to the noise and din that I had experienced in the night clubs.

Most clubs had a resident act to start off the proceedings. Some of the residents were often better entertainers than the guests appearing for the evening, and should have become well known on the circuit in their own right.

We used to enjoy a good night at the 'Pigot Arms,' in Pattingham, Shropshire. I still have a recording of a gig performed there one evening. It was here at the Pigot, that around 1974, I first met Penny, my future wife. She helped the girl who ran the club, Lynn Greenaway, by collecting the entrance fee on the door. Gone is the folk club that used to be held in the upper room, all they have now is a singers night, an open mike affair. How music venues have changed. It's funny to think of the many great names who performed at the club, and I feel sad that many are no longer with us, and those that are, are getting old or have retired. Bah!

Penny and I were friends for a long time before I developed a glint in my eye, but it gave us an opportunity to develop mutual trust. We got on really well, life was fun, and we both felt we could make a go of it. In 1978, we bought a house together and moved in. That was almost forty years ago. It is fair to say, that it was a constant battle with Penny's mother, right up to the time when she became too ill to look after herself, and needed to be moved into a care home. She did not want us to get together and made it quite clear that she would not give me the 'drippings off her nose!' As far as she was concerned, I was not good enough to marry her daughter. This would lead to some very serious problems later in life, and also when she refused to attend our wedding. Despite her feelings towards me, we carried on with all our own arrangements and married in 1983. We held the reception at 'The Pigot Arms,' for old time's sake, and had a great time surrounded by our friends, who only wished us well.

Me and Penny, at our Wedding in 1983

Authors Collection

Scene Four

Pack up all my cares and woe

About this time, I found myself with very little money and was forced to make a serious decision; should I carry on with my musical career? By now it appeared that I was not making much progress, and after all, we were all getting older and music tastes were changing. The folk scene seemed to virtually evaporate overnight. I don't know why. Perhaps people met their future partners at a club and settled down; perhaps we took it all for granted.

I felt that it was time to find a proper job with a regular salary. It's OK for a single man to enjoy a nomadic life, but that life was not for Penny, we had travelled enough. Now I had to take a different road............

The same actor friend, Graham, who had first suggested that I take my guitar to a folk club was also experiencing the fickle nature of the business himself. He, and a couple of pals from stage school, had managed to secure work in children's theatre and walk on parts in a TV show called 'Crossroads,' - you remember the wobbly sets! On one occasion, an actor called

Simon, had to play the part of a man at the bar ordering a drink. There were so many takes for the main actors, that the poor man nearly died of dehydration before they let him and the other extras have a cuppa! There's not much joy or money in this type of work, and it appeared that their acting careers were not going to progress much further. Graham and Simon were about to pack it in, whilst fortunately, Jeffrey Holland went for an audition, and landed a part in a comedy sitcom set in a holiday camp, called Hi Di Hi!, - and did quite well.

Graham was now working in a retail store. He said it was, 'Just like show business, we have to 'sparkle' for the customers,' - typical actor! After vouching for me to his employer, he helped me to secure a position with the same company.

Music gradually fell by the wayside, as I became used to the regular money. I did occasionally perform with a couple of different ones, but my heart was not really in it anymore; anyway, I had to be up for work each morning, no lay ins now!

Mike Lamb and I had a few good laughs and enjoyed the short time we performed together. He did a really good routine about how they trained medieval doctors, (well that's what he told me) by pointing out the body parts to the assembled students. There has been many a shy and embarrassed young lady, who wished that she had not so readily volunteered, when Mike requested someone from the audience to join him in his demonstration.

Entering into the world of business, I quickly moved on from the shop floor to a position within a high street chain of electronics retailers, based at their head offices in the Midlands. I was responsible for half the U.K., and several overseas territories, and my brief was to develop a dealer network of retail shops. I threw myself into the job, virtually at the expense of everything else.

I found out Gerry Lockran had been ill when he wrote to me, saying that he had been the victim of a stroke and a heart attack. Gerry always seemed so fit and well, so I expected him to fully recover. Along with Biffo Griffiths, I went to see him at his home. He and his wife Bobby made us lunch and he went on to tell me of his determination to beat the stroke. The feeling in one arm was taking a long time to come back, and he was beginning to think that he may never be able to perform again.

This annoyed him so much, after all, it had been his life for so many years, and his audience loved him, and he loved them. The thought of never seeing them again was very upsetting for him. He was going to beat this and had started to learn to play the guitar left handed! I cannot imagine the determination that this must have taken. We said our fond farewells, and I said the usual thing that we all say, 'I'll be in touch.'

Although I was by now making a success of developing the dealer programme, I was just as poor as when I was a jobbing musician, except that now I was poor in a company car and a suit. I had a job, job was the word, 'Just Over Broke' and as I said before, the money was appalling, and Penny and I were going through a serious financial crisis. We had moved house a couple of years ago, and then the mortgage interest rates went up to a staggering 15%! Each month we were slipping a bit deeper into the mire. We had to watch every 'farthing.' Jobs were very hard to find, so you had to hang on to the one you had. The company directors and senior managers used this as a stick to beat the workforce, much the same as is happening now. I would not wish the stress of being in that situation on any hard working family. The outcome was that we would not use the heating or telephone, unless it was absolutely necessary, and turned off all unnecessary lights in the house. We were financially under the cosh; consequently I did not contact Gerry for a while. Working hard and long hours, another different road was stretching out before me.

I began to build up happy relationships with my dealer network and had some wonderful Grand Openings around the country. In some ways, it was rather like show business, when one appeared with the local mayor and press to publicise the new store. A couple of stories from this 'stage' in my life, will show that selling was not that far removed from my performing days.

At a 'Grand Opening' in Tiverton, Devon, we completely blocked the town with excited shoppers; much to the consternation of Roy and Fleur Hart, the new proprietors. A policeman pushing through the throngs on a horse was the only way to move people along! In Daventry too we had a cracker, when a man I came to admire, Mike Griffin, decided to invest with us. Again we stopped the town; the Lord Mayor, positively beaming in his gold chain, delighted the crowds by handing out free torches. It's fair to say that I was very fond of my dealers and the role consumed a great deal of my time.

Eventually, some months later, I finally rang Gerry one Saturday evening. A young lady answered the phone and I asked to speak to the great man.

'Whose calling?' she asked,

'Tell him it's Pete Shakespear.'

'You haven't heard?' she said,

'Heard what?'

'Gerry passed away two months ago!'

I felt like I had been hit with a hammer. I don't think I said very much except that I thanked her, said I was sorry, and slowly returned the receiver back onto its cradle. I was inconsolable. Even now, after all these years, I still feel a sense of grief; it just comes over me when I play his albums sometimes. Had I become mean? Had I become uncaring? Couldn't I have spared a quid to call the best friend I ever had in show business?

To this day, I curse the company I worked for at that time

for keeping us so poor, I should have told them to stuff it; I would have in my younger days, but now I was in debt and had a mortgage. I was over a barrel! I hate the fact that massive profits are made by companies on the backs of honest, decent, hardworking people, and this is what it can lead to. How I regret not keeping in touch with Gerry, a lesson in life I will never forget.

As the years went by, I did quite well in sales management, holding a succession of senior positions, and eventually, because of my experience, I was invited to become a Fellow of the Institute of Sales and Marketing; training some good people along the way. One day, quite by chance, through having to collect some paperwork for a Dutch supplier, I found myself being offered a job by the C.E.O. and Managing Director of a newly formed company.

This new set up was captained by a man who once owned one of the most famous nightclubs in the world, 'The Golden Torch' in Hanley, Staffordshire. The club was well known for its live shows, great music and DJ's, and also for its 'all nighters.' The club is still revered to this day, and a plaque marks the place where the building stood that had such an influence on 'Northern Soul' fans throughout the world.

Chris Burton had just started a new company which was wholesaling the new kid on the block, Compact Disc. The investment group, Parkfield, had injected new venture capital and Chris invited me to join him. Chris was a ball of energy and a great mentor; we shared some exciting times together, creating new ideas and business strategies to take our market share of the new medium. Within months, we had taken the company sales into many millions of pounds. Following our success with Compact Disc, we began the move into the rental video film market, supplying many major high street retail chains and record shops. Parkfield Entertainment became in a short time, a major player, financing films such as 'The Krays' with Gary and Martin Kemp and Billie Whitelaw, and a television series called 'Lonesome Dove,' starring Robert Duval, Tommy Lee Jones and Danny Glover. It all seemed to be going well, but I was soon to be led down a completely different road.

After the birth of our son, my wife's health began to deteriate quite badly. Although she had had rheumatoid arthritis since the age of eleven, the damn thing flared up alarmingly several months after a tetanus injection at the well woman clinic! I now found myself having to take early retirement to care for her needs and take more responsibility in the upbringing of our son. As the stairs were becoming a problem for her, we moved to a bungalow in Cornwall, hopefully to improve Penny's condition and general health. For all of us I guess, life is about different roads and how we deal with the journey.

As I said, music is in the blood, and now during my spare

time, such as it was, I began working on the idea of marketing a new album. We talked with several agents about releasing the album in the Far Eastern market and Russia, and extensively promoted the album to see if any interest could be found, but alas, ... the music industry had changed, things had moved on.

I appreciated the time and effort put forth by Kate and Larry Rushton; we spent many hours in their studio, they were a great encouragement in putting the album together. Larry is a brilliant guitarist and producer and Kate can harmonise with the best in the business. Together they could put on a fabulous show aimed at an older audience. I learned that Larry has had one of his songs recorded by Engelbert Humperdinck for his album, and another is being performed in the 'Dreamboats and Petticoats' show in the West End. I really feel happy when hard working, time served, writers and musicians finally get through, although it is more by luck now than judgement.

I have to be honest and say, that over the years, I have had my chances and possibly, could have made more of them - as a few of these stories will testify. Put it down to bad business decisions, stupidity, lack of confidence, whatever, but you are never out of the race, ... unless you stop.

The last touring gigs I did were when I, and another guitarist, James Davey, opened the show for Raymond Froggatt during the 'Chasin' Songs' tour. Ray has written some great songs, recorded by some of show businesses biggest stars. It was after many years that I bumped into Ray and his long time guitarist, H Cain, in a music shop in Shropshire. His words were,

'Blinkin' 'ek Shakey, we thought you were dead!'

I believe that Ray is a truly great professional and it was a privilege to help out, but I did feel a little out of place, - after all it was Ray's audience - and quite right too!

The journey has at times been a very rough one. I am sad to say that the folk scene is not what it was, but I am so glad that there appears to be a renaissance, and now that our duty has been done to bring up the kids and provide for our old age, (let's face it the government won't,) many old folkies are returning to hear the beautiful music of their youth, - and I hear that Chris Burton is organising 'Torch' reunions. You can't keep good music or a good man down!

Looking back, at least I can say that I gave it a good shot. I am disappointed that I could not have made more of my chances, although I have had the privilege of meeting and listening to many wonderful artistes, and through tolerance and understanding, had my life enriched by their friendship. I came from a very poor background, surrounded by people who felt beaten before they started. When I had the courage to break out, only to be confronted by the world full on, it totally knocked me sideways, as I didn't have much confidence to begin with; but thanks to some good pals and eventually, a good wife, we are here - still standing.

Although I still get stage fright - amazing to think that the nervous feeling has never left me - yet, if the first chords ring true and the first notes of the voice hit the clock, then I am away. You would hopefully never know that inside my jeans, my poor knees wobble like a jelly! As I have said previously, I really hate growing older, and whilst I acknowledge that mutton dressed as lamb is not very appealing, I believe that we should make the best of what we have.

Strangely, some people I've met seem to take pleasure in growing older. I was speaking to a poor excuse for a man recently, about in his late fifties. He obviously didn't exercise or read much, and he was saying that he preferred a bacon sandwich to a pretty girl or intimacy, proudly declaring, 'Well, most blokes have gone off it by the time they're fifty!' Surely that's not all there is? Is that it, really? Fifty, and it's all over? No ambition left, all zest for life taken wings .... I don't think so! True, when I stand in the spotlight, the top of my head is beginning to resemble a car headlight, and I can't eat a pizza at least twelve hours before going to bed, and my eyes are now getting a bit dim, - but everything else works, including my love of knowledge; particularly, in recent years, my interest in computer programmes like C.A.D. Surely, if you switch your brain off, you may as well crawl away into a hole - not me! Don't you fall prey to it either!

I recently walked out onto a stage and was temporarily blinded by the spotlights. I find that if I take my specs off, everybody's face becomes a pink blob; I can see my crib sheet clearly, but then I cannot make eye contact with my audience. Some people might have a suggestion as to why my eyesight is now fading! But never mind.

I hope that so far I have entertained you, dear reader, but most of all that I have encouraged you to think positively. In every bad situation there is always the glimmer of success, the trick I guess is to be able to see it.

I heard a great saying once: 'Most people do not recognise opportunity, because it's disguised as hard work!' - Please make sure that the person this applies to is not you!

And another one I like, - you may have often heard people say, 'Oh, you're lucky ... !' What? - Remember, luck means,

Labour, Under the **Correct Knowledge,**

so you've gotta be in it to even stand a hope of winning!!

Scene Five

The Saturday morning knock, or The Jehovah's Witness Years

'Tell a lie once and all your truths become questionable'
Mufti Ismail Menk

I cannot conclude this story of my life without tackling the very thorny issue of religion; after all it had affected my life for many years! What a person wishes to believe is very definitely up to them, after all we are all born free; thousands of men like my granddad fought for us to be so. We have a right to choose for ourselves, but it's when we think that we have an insight into 'ultimate truth,' that things boil over and we can begin to impose our idea of 'truth' and our way of looking at things on to others. You only have to take a peek at history to see the damage that religion has done to the human race.

I have always attempted to keep my beliefs to myself when arranging bookings and dealing with other show business professionals, but when it came to family it was a different thing. Sadly, I now find myself having to sincerely apologise to many friends, business colleagues, acquaintances and family members, for the foolish things I was persuaded to believe.

My journey of wanting to know why, where, and what we are here for, really began when as a child, the wonderful lady that lived next door to us passed away.

Mr and Mrs Ball, (Ted and Elsie) were the epitome of good neighbourliness. Having no children of their own, they would bring us presents from their annual holiday in Blackpool and Mrs Ball would give us a few sweets every day; truly the finest people. She was a gentle Christian person, Church every Sunday, non judgemental and forgiving, as was Mr Ball. I loved the smell of his pipe smoke when he would enjoy it out in the small yard at the rear of the house, I think it was St Bruno tobacco, (I don't think he was allowed to smoke indoors) and when he chatted over the fence with my father and I was around, he would always include me in the conversation.

Not many people had a television in those days, but every year Mr Ball would ask my father, my brother and me to watch the Cup Final with him around at their house. A great man.

Things began to go wrong after Mrs Ball's sister had contracted cancer and died quite suddenly. In Mrs Ball's mind she too, believed she was dying. I don't know why, I think the menopause was under way. People didn't speak of this in those days. I can only assume, but as any mature person will know, the monthly cycles can become horrendous as a lady gets older;

possibly because of this she convinced herself that she too had cancer. She did not. She basically starved herself to death; she took to her bed, refused to get up, and after several weeks, she died. I remember it was on a Sunday afternoon, a beautiful hot summer's day. Days later, as I watched her coffin being carried out of the front door, a large white cross of flowers on top, and placed inside the big black limousine by the pall bearers, I awoke to the fact that that was where we are all going to end up, and naturally I felt afraid, even at a very young age.

We were taught Bible stories at Wood End Infants School, but I could never see the sense of a God making something beautiful and then leaving it to perish. My feelings deepened as I got older and began to see the awful deeds carried out by man in the name of God and religion. It left me wanting to have nothing to do with it. I even told Willy's wife Molly, that she was silly getting involved with such things when she became a Jehovah's Witness, but perhaps it was understandable, when you consider what had happened with Andrew, she must have been beside herself with grief and only wanted him back. Little did I realise at the time that I too would eventually make the same mistake

I had, for some years, been seriously wondering about life due to another strange incident that happened around 1965. On a balmy Saturday evening during late summer, my father, brother and a school friend of my brother's, Paul Johnson were sitting outside in the garden appreciating the cooler night air. Whilst my father was having a quiet cigarette, we let our eyes wander around the beautiful starry heavens. There was no moon that night and not a cloud in the sky. Without warning and with no noise, what we thought was a star began to grow and expand, within seconds reaching the size of a car headlamp, glowing intensely. We all watched mesmerised! Suddenly, two other dim stars from different parts of the sky began to glow, then they also grew to the size of a car headlamp. The three lights very slowly moved toward each other to form a triangle, dimmed again, then shot off in different directions at incredible speed. No noise, no vapour trail, and no flashing navigation lights, besides, I doubt that any craft even to this day could move so fast. We all sat staring upward, open mouthed. My father, a tough character, immediately ordered us,

'Get into the house boys!'

What it was I know not, but it got me wondering. When I have related this event to others over the years, one realised that many have had a similar experience. The question remained .... What on earth was it?

Many years later, when I had befriended Pat and Bryan and a lovely bloke called Roland, we used to talk into the wee small hours about life, and although we exchanged some heated points of view, we nevertheless all had the same interest and curiosity. I began to read the books of Erich Von Daniken and others, who expressed an alternative theory as to the origin of life on earth. I firmly convinced myself that his theory was possibly the truth. It seemed to me to be as good as any other explanation of how we appeared on earth.

This led to requesting Mr Daniken to appear at The Civic Hall in Wolverhampton to speak to us and an assembled audience, including the local Astronomical Society.

Promoted by Bryan, he was to present a talk and a slide show on the evidence, entitled, 'Was God an Astronaut?' I thought we had found the answer, or at least were on the right track, and I became seriously interested in what he had to say.

Some months later, it was on a Saturday morning, I became aware of loud voices and swear words flying around the hallway down stairs. I dragged myself from my room to investigate the source. There stood a man who had called to 'bring us the good news.' Unfortunately he had met my sister, who was giving him a severe chastising. I intervened to enquire what on earth was going on and reminded her that we do not speak to people like that; whereupon she left us to it. I said,

'Look mate, what do you want?'

He said that all he had asked the lady was, who she thought ruled the earth? I replied that I was not interested, and that if there were such a person then surely it would be the devil, judging by the way people behaved. He said that the Bible taught that this was so, and promptly thrust a Bible in my face and pointed out a passage of scripture. I was surprised, not by his action, but the fact that there were such words in the Bible; my immediate thoughts were, why has no one ever taught me these things? He politely asked me if I would like to know more? I said yes, and agreed to have a weekly discussion of the scriptures.

This of course, led me to a study of what I thought was the Bible, but now I know was really a study of one of the many Jehovah's Witness teaching aids designed to turn your thinking and reasoning to their own ideas and doctrine! Anyway, truth is that I began to be drawn in and started to look forward to God's Kingdom ruling and setting all matters straight. This was just before 1975, ring any bells?

Although all the Jehovah's Witnesses I had begun to associate with, were fully convinced that 1975 would bring about the end of the world, I had reservations and made my views known. Of course, they now requested that I not attend their weekly meetings anymore and they felt that after six months of study, I should have by now given myself over to them. Therefore, I left off my studies and attempted to move on with my music. Fast forward a few years years later to 1982..............

A knock came on the door of our new home; on opening it I was surprised and pleased to see that it was Pat Hannon whom I had not seen for several years. By now, you all know that I treasured Pat as my friend, so I invited him in. He excitedly began to explain,

'Shakey, I have just what you need!'

'What?' I said.

Pat replied, 'You have always wanted to plant 'taters' (potatoes) - meaning that all I ever wanted was a peaceful life and to enjoy the earth. He was right. He, of course, had also received the Saturday morning knock and was well along in his conversion to be a Jehovah's Witness, as were his wife, and his brother and sister-in-law. When he explained himself, I immediately exhorted that he not get involved with them, and told him how I went through the 1975 debacle. Pat told me that they had indeed got it wrong and that it was only a rumour started by the local JW's, but now it really was the truth that he and his family were learning. He convinced me to sit in with him on his family study, just to see what was going on, I could ask as many questions as I liked, all would be answered.

By now, Penny and me had set up home, and I wondered if it really was possible to never have to be parted from the ones we love; a natural feeling surely, but one that leaves humans open to manipulation from many sources, including and perhaps foremost, religion. Anyway, Penny and I began to trust Pat, and we started a study together. This led to us both being baptised after about eighteen months of learning, or should I say, indoctrination!

I found myself constantly observing the hypocritical things that went on within the congregations, and to be honest not liking what I saw.

Many of the young Witnesses would often be seen drunk or taking drugs and mooning (showing their bum,) outside nightclubs around Birmingham; they could be very offensive and one club even posted a notice that Jehovah's Witnesses were barred. But, after voicing my concerns, I was convinced by Elders (the appointed men in the congregation supposed to shepherd the flock) that 'Gods Organisation' was clean, and was also persuaded to believe that this behaviour had not gone unnoticed and sooner or later they would have to face the music. Little did I understand, until long after the events, that it was often Elders' children who were misbehaving, and daddy and mommy were turning a blind eye.

Firmly convinced that the Bible was true, and by now converted into believing that 'The Governing Body' of Jehovah's Witnesses were 'God's chosen channel of communication; my wife and I soldiered on.

Eventually, admittedly after many years, the hypocrisy got to me. I had heard and seen enough of Elders having it away with female members of the congregation, enough of their young people on anti-depressant pills, enough suicides, divorces and unhappy people. I had seen too many great human beings wasting their life; kids that dreamed of being doctors, vets, nurses, sports coaches and footballers. Talented people like Peter Knowles, the Wolves footballer, who would have possibly played for England in the 1970 Mexico World Cup squad, and the great musician Ken Price, who I heard had been reduced to playing his guitar in the back kitchen. I was told that his family were forbidding him from playing out, and that he should not seek fame! Good grief, we only wanted to play music!

I have watched them throw their lives away for a lie! God's kingdom still hadn't come, the generation that saw 1914 was gone, and by now JW's were teaching some foolishness about overlapping generations. I began to doubt the things I had learned. Surely, if this was God's chosen organisation, then shouldn't we have been the happiest people ever to walk the earth? I now find myself weeping as I write after seeing so much unhappiness and mind control. No, we should never fritter away our precious moments in life by listening to losers, waste our time abusing our health through using drugs, or being with people who are rude, violent and manipulative.

Most of the JW children, poor souls, leave school (that is if they even attended one, as home education is encouraged) without any qualifications, only to become window washers, cleaners and toilet attendants, having been convinced that their time is best spent unpaid, knocking doors.

Life's too short to mess with, but at least I had lived a bit and 'been round the block,' before I got involved. I really wish that the authorities would get on their case, but the mind control is very subtle and if one dares to question their authority and doctrine then a barrage of abuse is unleashed, and if you don't give in to it, then you are hauled into 'the back room' and warned to shut up or go! If it appears that you are not towing the party line, you may be shunned by other members of the congregation who deem you to be 'bad association.' This can embarrass and frighten you into keeping quiet or dropping your complaint. Should you decide to leave the organisation, or fade away, or if you have the misfortune to be disfellowshipped (excommunicated) for some 'sin,' then you will be totally shunned by all your former 'Christian family!' If one disassociates oneself from the organisation, then you are considered to be an 'apostate.' The 'Watchtower' policy is then to view you as dead! The love they say they have is, I am afraid to say, conditional on your following 'The Society' without question. If I had known this first, I assure you dear reader, I would have had more sense than to get involved with this cult. There must be thousands of Jehovah's Witnesses sitting at their meetings and listening to all that twaddle, but who are afraid to speak out for fear of being shunned by their friends or family. An organisation built on fear, and not love, cannot surely survive, can it? I wonder how many Jehovah's Witnesses must be leading 'double' lives.

It all unravelled one night, after Penny had gone out to one of the meetings. I had stayed at home, having missed a few meetings, because of developing a heavy cold. I was also feeling very uneasy about the whole affair of lies, cover ups and hypocrisy, having also had a run-in with a long established family of JW's, whom I had accused of lying to a travelling overseer about me and my family. All we were doing was asking for answers and expressing doubts - they wanted us out.

Jehovah's Witnesses are taught that the whole world is lying in the power of the devil and we should have nothing to do with it. Furthermore, anyone who is not a Jehovah's Witness will die at Armageddon, God's holy war against the wicked! Some have been warned never to look at websites such as the 'British Museum' or to read encyclopaedias on history, as they consider them to be 'apostate' and not of God. The only website they are officially allowed to seek information from is their own. This is obviously so that they can hide their manipulation of scripture, history and dates. Their man made rules also include a perverse view of education. The children of JW's are told not to even consider university. I promise that I did not know this when I first agreed to join them, if I had I would have asked them to prove their point of view from the Bible. I never questioned their authority of the scriptures, and so to be honest, I let myself be misled. I must have just followed blindly, until it came to the education of my son. In this, I went firmly against their stupid teaching about education and really upset the applecart, opening the biggest can of worms I could ever have imagined.

It has only been a few years since I became computer literate; I attended a Microsoft course a few years ago and with help from my son and plenty of practise, I can now find my way around a computer, and guess where it led me?? Yes, the internet!! Oh, how stupid I feel now that I have discovered the true facts about Jehovah's Witnesses. Talk about being duped, being deceived, I can pick em' can't I!?

Here are just a few of the things which I have uncovered, and incidentally, I requested in my resignation letter to them that if I was wrong, would someone kindly put me straight. To date no one has been able to, or even tried, they treat us as dead, just because we asked questions!

C.T. Russell the founder of the organisation known as International Bible Students (IBSA) believed in Pyramidology, the study of the Pyramids of Egypt. In his series of books entitled, 'Studies in the Scriptures,' he expounded through diagrams that the pyramids were God's stone witnesses and from the length of the internal passages within the pyramid the date of Christ's second coming could be accurately worked out.

Because his predictions didn't happen on time, in successive reprints of his book he changed the date for the beginning of the millennium reign of Christ from 1874, in 1904, to 1914 in the 1910 edition of his book.

One account I read, stated that he blamed the change in date from one edition to another, on the poor bugger who had got his scaling sizes out when transposing the measurements wrongly from Russell's drawings. Always blaming someone else is a common theme amongst these people.

A judge in a court case involving C.T. Russell and his wife, accused him of fraud and being a liar! So much for God's chosen one!

The case of the miracle wheat is interesting too.

Russell was accused of making huge profits from a strain called 'Miracle Wheat,' which supposedly was able to give a bigger yield than ordinary wheat.

The Brooklyn Daily Eagle reported Russell's alleged fraud, whereupon Russell took them to court claiming libel. The 'Eagle' declared that:

'at the trial it will show that 'Pastor' Russell's religious cult is nothing more than a money-making scheme.'

Russell lost the case, ah well, we know now!

In another account, once, so the story goes, when caught by his wife kissing a young female Bethel worker in a broom cupboard, C.T. stated that, 'He was only trying to give the sister some spiritual encouragement!' He died on a train on Halloween in 1916, some say under mysterious circumstances. He gave instructions that on his death he was to be buried in a

Roman toga! and like the founder of the Mormons, Joseph Smith, who allegedly was shot and murdered through revealing too many secrets, he too was apparently a Freemason. Russell's stone Pyramid in the Freemason graveyard at Rosemount, Pennsylvania, probably attests to this, try Google Earth and see it for yourself!

The next President of The Watchtower, 'Judge' Rutherford claimed that 'Millions Now Living Will Never Die.' He published a book of the same name and in it stated as such. He prophesied to having divine knowledge that the resurrection of the dead would start in 1925 and embarked upon a nationwide tour declaring this as fact.

Hundreds of thousands of Witnesses sold houses, businesses and land, thinking he was right. They donated their money to pay for ministers to travel worldwide, preaching their brand of Bible understanding. They were zealous to save the human race from destruction.

Rutherford started the largest Bible, book and tract printing organisation in the world at that time. He ordered that a man must be clean shaven and women were only to wear skirts, not trousers; and he sent them packing with nothing but books to sell, so that they could feed themselves; calling them colporteurs and reminding them of the urgency of their work. At the same time, the 'Judge' had himself been living in the lap of luxury in a mansion, which he called 'Beth Sarim' in sunny

California, built especially by him using Watchtower funds. He claimed it was built for the returning 'Princes of the Bible!' During the prohibition period, he lived on the best food and finest wine, served by members of the Bethel (house of God) and he owned not one, but two Cadillacs! See a pattern here anyone! 1925 came and went; many were left disappointed and penniless, the Watchtower having taken it all

Rutherford too had the indignity of being exposed for shabby behaviour, including drunkenness. (Please search out the letter by Olin Moyle who successfully sued Rutherford for slander.) He was also a supporter of Adolph Hitler, until Hitler wouldn't listen to him; eventually Rutherford published sarcastic cartoons which turned the Fuhrer against the Witnesses. He died lonely; it is said only four people attended his funeral. His body is reportedly buried under the concrete floor of the garage at Beth Sarim.

The next deception was where I came in, and eventually fell for it, - the lie about 1975. I had always been told and believed, and even defended the fact, that the Jehovah's Witnesses never prophesied the world's end in 1975. I can now state that they positively did!!

I read a transcription of the then Vice President of the Watchtower Bible and Tract Society, Freddie Franz, speaking at a Special World-wide talk at Dodger Stadium, Los Angeles, California on the 10th of February 1975, stating plainly that the world would end on September 5th 1975! He tub thumped that anyone who dared to disagree would laugh on the other side of their face, including newspaper reporters who were holding in derision this wonderful 'truth' which he was declaring!

The Bible tells us that anyone who claims to speak in God's name and the saying does not come true, he is a false prophet deserving of death. From all this evidence we can simply state that, because of the many false prophecies that Jehovah's Witnesses and their Governing Body have made over many years, they are not God's chosen people, if anything they are from their father the devil, he too was a liar! I understand that even now, one of their silly sod Governing Body members is claiming that, 'There is more evidence for God's Kingdom beginning in 1914 than there is for gravity, electricity and wind!' Oh pleeease, please, lock him up!!

The most shocking revelation for me though (as if things could be worse) was the fact that millions of dollars were being paid out in damages to ceertain Jehovah's Witnesses who as children had been sexually abused whilst still within a congregation. Can you believe it? Jehovah's Witnesses can't, because members of their Governing Body have told them that whatever the press says is all lies, except of course when it appears to be in their favour! Recently, a woman in America, Candace Conti, was awarded 25 million dollars (reduced on appeal to 11 million dollars I heard) for sexual abuse by a congregation Elder, and as recently as October 2014, 13 million dollars has been awarded to a man who was abused in a San Diego Congregation - but they will probably appeal, oh my goodness!

Although the Witnesses state that they abhor such things, the book, 'Shepherd the Flock of God,' (only given to Elders and classed as secret and not to be read by their wives or any other members of the congregation) states that, on receiving a complaint from a member of a congregation of abuse, 'You should immediately call the branch office for direction' - hold on a bit, this is a crime, why are they not instructed to immediately call the police!

The Royal Commission in Australia, appointed to investigate the claims of cases of abuse within Jehovah's Witnesses, are still collecting evidence, there are so many! Bloody Hell! who on earth had I gotten involved with!! Add to this my discovery of their ten year membership of the UN as an NGO, (they had taught us the UN was a tool of the devil) their alleged dealing in hedge funds, their flip flop changes of Bible understanding and I am afraid my world collapsed.

There is an old saying isn't there, 'Follow the money!' They are now selling off property for millions of dollars and yet still pointing out to their members how important it is to send regular donations, including the children's ice cream money, think I'm joking?!!

When I first started to uncover these things, Penny thought I had gone mad and refused to believe me. Thankfully, she finally trusted me enough for me to show her the information I had gleaned; shocked, she too stopped attending meetings. Even today, I tell ones why I no longer associate and they say oh well, there are bad people everywhere! What!! No, it appears that this organisation is covering over some very serious things, making false prophecies and giving a false hope to what are really lovely people on the whole, who only want a better world. When one of Willy's children contacted me recently, to see if it was true that I had disassociated myself from the JW's, and I confirmed that I had, the convivial atmosphere changed. As I began to outline some of my discoveries, the reply was,

'Well, I've known these things for years, I am a researcher!'

My anger almost got the better of me, I exclaimed,

'You mean you knew, and said nothing! You do not have the integrity your father gave you and you should be ashamed!'

Surely it's true isn't it, I mean, how can anyone follow something that they know to be definitely wrong! It's like asking a salesperson to sell a product they do not believe in; a waste of time!

Jehovah's Witnesses, or jw.org as they are now known, are beginning to spend much time and resources in debunking the so called 'apostate lies.' However, millions are now waking up to their falsehood. I am afraid the World Wide Web appears to have been their undoing. Over the years I have seen lovely gentle people pass away, whilst still believing that the Kingdom was coming 'soon.'

What can I say, I have been silly, and there are still millions of others who are being duped as we speak, I can only try and encourage them to use their freedom wisely. In reality though, no one can wake anyone else up, we have to see it for ourselves and admit that we have doubts, and not be afraid to investigate why we feel the way we do. Can't they see that if any house is constructed on a poor foundation it is bound to collapse eventually? There is probably much, much, more to uncover and I would encourage all students to check every word these charlatans say, ask questions, check it for yourself and use the internet, the information is out there, not covered over as it used to be. A hard lesson learned!

Don't judge me too harshly please, all I ever wanted was to see my loved ones again, see an end to war and suffering, and live in peace. I have such a curious mind, that if I lived a hundred lifetimes I would never learn enough. This, I suppose, leaves me open to being deceived, and God knows I am not perfect, but liars and deceivers are not the sort of folks I want to be associated with. Where I went wrong was assuming that JW's were right. My commission was, on pain of death, to tell as many people as I could that if they did not follow what 'God's chosen channel' said, they would die at Armageddon. I certainly didn't want anyone destroyed. All this judging others is wrong, no one has the right. How can it be so when we learn that 'God is love.' I suppose all things being considered, that's what we all need, just love ..... whoever we are.

So, there you have it dear reader, if you are looking for the answer to life and all things, I don't know, I thought I did, but it's patently obvious that I don't. I am still unsure what ghosts and UFOs are!

I respect anyone who has a faith and a belief system which brings them hope and comfort, I will never judge you, but as for me I will never again have anything to do with religion or answer the Saturday morning knock at the door. To have had such a positive belief shattered, takes many months or even years to recover from, and some never really get over it. Thankfully, we are getting back on our feet and are now able to talk about it and smile again. I often say to Penny........

'You don't drown by falling in the water, you drown if you stay there.'

I didn't feel that it was appropriate to discuss this subject when I wrote the original 'Different Roads' but I was wrong. I see now, because of the things I have discovered, that I owe it to other Jehovah's Witnesses and their Bible students, to speak up. They may be suspecting something is wrong with this church's teachings, and want to leave the organisation, but stay in the shadows in fear. Take my advice:

'Don't stay in the shadows in fear, step into the light in faith!'

Really that advice can apply in many situations. Dear Leonard Cohen wrote,

'There is a crack in everything, that's how the light gets in.'

If anyone is considering studying the Bible with Jehovah's Witnesses, please don't!! .... run a mile!!!

There has to be more to life than meets the eye, from the goo, to the zoo, to you, doesn't seem right, but I don't know the answer, you will have to work it out for yourself! I do know that this lot haven't got it right, far from it! For me, I feel now, religion has caused most of the problems in this world and is best left alone.

Postscript:

In conclusion, I guess it's time to bring my story of 'Different Roads' to a fitting end. The journey has been unusual in the fact that I worked with many major acts in the soul and reggae world and made a surprising change of direction when I moved to folk music. I then had the privilege to meet and work with more fine human beings, and it was wonderful to perform in front of such lovely audiences too. From there the road led into the world of retailing Electronics, Compact Disc and the Film Industry, talk about variety!

I would though be concerned if a young person were to try the show business route today. As a great friend of mine, who himself has been at it for as long as I have, said, 'Show business is a bag of dung' (I'm being polite here for his sake.) All most of us ever wanted to do was make music; we didn't expect to be ripped off virtually every step of the way. Some of us nearly lost our life in the process, and with so many leaving us so early for whatever reason, it begs the question, was it all worth it? Well, if it wasn't for music, I would not have had so many life changing experiences, and no doubt I would not have moved far from the village where I was born.

Some folks, usually with little real talent, if they smell

success, soon have their hand out, or in your pocket. There are those, of course, who have made a fortune from the business, but not alas, the thousands of ordinary boys and girls who entered with starry eyes and great hopes. But please, let's enjoy our music, plonk a guitar, join a choir, sing in the chorus; it brings people together and helps make true friends who will last a lifetime, and always remember you are never alone with a good song! But, don't take it too seriously. I know that throughout our nation there must be many ordinary boys and girls who were musicians, dancers and DJ's who have a tale to tell, I am certainly not unique.

I have to thank those in the industry who have shown me good manners. Just to acknowledge a letter of proposal would be an encouragement in itself, but it's like hens teeth to receive any communication once the padded envelope is in the post box. The stupid thing is that show business gets into the blood and it's difficult to stop writing and wanting to perform and meet new friends.

I hope the website will help me keep in touch with friends old and new, so look out for it and if you see us around, for goodness sake, say hello!

When I look back and see how the world has changed and think of some of the people I have met along the way in my musical career, I have come to the conclusion that life is too short, but I still want to learn more and do something more than just vegetate.

May I thank Dec Cluskey, of The Bachelors fame, and Bruce Welch from the Shadows who kindly rang, even though what was proposed would not have worked out. Good manners are rare in the business and I really appreciated the calls.

Thanks also go to Billy Howe of 'Lost Wolverhampton' for reminding me of the chippy in Snow Hill, and Paul Townsend of 'Bristolpast' for letting me use his photo of the Bamboo Club.

May I thank Victoria Wallett for editing and Pete Junior for his hard work sorting out my computer glitches. Without both of them I could not have completed the book.

Speaking of acknowledgements, some people will wonder why I haven't mentioned their names. It may be that I don't recall a situation we were involved in together, or it may be that I simply can't remember a name, and for that I can only apologise. However, I may have chosen not to remember the ones who, instead of accepting the crumbs off the cake and being helpful and sharing when we were having it rough, wanted not just the crumbs but a complete slice, and in some cases, the whole cake. I love generous people, generous in spirit and with their time and talent, but the mean, selfish and self centred I prefer to forget.

Isn't it strange that the moment I decide to put pen to paper something happens. What I mean is this: for years now my time as a musician had been becoming a distant memory. After asking Steryl Williams' daughter Molvia if she knew if any members of the family had any photographs that I could use in my book, she suggested that I contact a local radio station who might be interested in broadcasting a programme about the history of the town, its musical history in particular.

The programme was called, 'Inside Tracks' and hosted by Pete Whitehouse. The guests are asked to pick ten songs that have influenced their life - picking just ten is really more difficult than it sounds. Pete very kindly asked me on to the programme, broadcasting to thousands of his listeners in the Midlands. Pete was kind and thoughtful as we discussed the music, the book, and my life in general. I wish to thank Pete for his invitation and professionalism. Since then, I have been invited to appear at several folk clubs. It's amazing the amount of interest now in the genre as the clubs spring up again. I recently had a surprise when after being off the scene for so many years, I popped into a club and caught the eye of someone who I thought I recognised. It was Jon Tame; he too had been told that I was dead!

Another huge surprise was when I had the opportunity to play a few numbers with Willy. It was on Molly and Willy's 40th wedding anniversary, the family had arranged a party for them and asked me to get together for old time's sake. It was the first time he had played since Andrew's death and we took several long weekends to work up to speed, but it was worth it, for one last time.

I was shocked, when one day in early spring of 2013, I received a telephone call out of the blue from my old long time musical partner Jon Tame, who I had bumped into just a few months earlier.

He related how his wife Sue had been severely injured whilst on a zebra crossing making her way to work at about 8:30am. She had received the full force of a car whose driver had not seen her and jumped the traffic. She had horrific injuries including both legs shattered, a broken pelvis and internal bleeding and was now in an induced coma. Jon wanted to know if I would be interested in helping with a fund raising concert for the Air Ambulance. Because of its rapid response it had undoubtedly saved the life of Sue, and of course I readily agreed to be on the bill.

Thanks to the website, I was exceedingly happy to have once again made contact with several treasured pals, including Tona and Scobie, we had many things to reminisce and smile about. But just as we began to renew our friendships tragedy has struck again.

On a truly sad note, my old pal Tona passed away on 23rd March 2016. He led a colourful life to say the least, from night club doorman to skipper of an ocean going yacht, to secretary of a chapter of the Harley-Davidson motorcycle club. On learning of his diagnosis, he rode up to see me on the Harley, (shaking the windows in the village where I now live) and to tell me of his determination to fight on, and how he was arranging a fund raising ride for the 'Help for Heroes' charity.

It reminded me once again that, like granddad, some of the poor lads were being treated harshly by the same government that wanted to waste them on the battlefield. I will treasure our friendship always.

My website includes a page with links to my book, 'Tales from the North Pole' that has had five star reviews and my autobiography published as a digital edition, I was assured that it was the modern way to go, we will see. I hope the revised version will be well received.

There is also a link to a local newspaper 'The Black Country Bugle' where I have an article published about the exploits of my grandfather during World War I, entitled, 'The Willenhall sailor that fought in the trenches.'

But sadly, I have now to call it a day, I feel a bit like a dinosaur and I am developing arthritis in my hands, so I want to spend my time relaxing awhile, caring for my family and my cat and going to a few holiday destinations that I had previously not visited due to commitments. I am showing all the signs of getting older, hair going white and thinning, thickening up around the waist, and having to admit that I have feet of clay, oh well life's a crapper!! Penny is coping with the debilitating arthritis as much as one can do, and enjoys flower arranging, nagging, and frying pan hurling! She is considering taking up pipe smoking and getting a mynah bird and teaching it to swear at me!

Pete Junior decided not to follow my wayward path and worked hard to win a First Class Honours Degree in Accountancy and Finance, as I said, without Pete's help I could not have completed the book, clever little bugger!

Dear me, ... is that the time already, ... gotta go! Time to feed the cat!!!

I hope you have enjoyed the tales of an ordinary jobbing musician, and perhaps it will spark some lively discussions, bringing to mind old friends, and the clubs, bands and musicians we knew, and maybe some of the musicians will remember the gear we used to use, and perhaps like me, will wish we had never sold it, oh well! So I leave you with an autograph that I promised to show you, it is one of my little treasures, the one that unknowingly helped to start me on the road to an interesting, if stressful, but always exciting musical career.

Authors Collection

The autograph of one of my all time favourite singers, The great Billy Fury.

keep kool,

Thanks for listening,

Pete.

The moon looks down.

I'm thinking that I dreamed and kissed again, the one that gave me love and life to me.

I know that I heard your voice, echo around my head,
And I just wanted to hear you say ...hello.
I'm still here waiting,

For I know it's true,
That until the end of time,
I'll still be missing you.

If only I, believe the things I do, then pity me life has no purpose too,
but that is not the way, for I know it's true,
And I'll have to wait until the time
When all things are made new,
And as I say a prayer, across the miles it flies,

In the sky the moon and you,
Look down on me and smile.

No I will not forget, for that is not my way,
just to see you once again I'm always living for that day,
So as I say my prayer, across the miles it flies,

In the sky the moon and you, look down on me and smile.

In the sky the moon and you, look down on me and smile
....

Night night, see you again soon.......

©Pete Shakespear

THE END

Different Roads is the autobiography of **Pete Shakespear.**

Now published as an updated version in 2017, 'Different Roads' includes new photographs, stories, anecdotes and a completely new chapter, the contents of which may surprise many.

Pete writes about growing up in the 1950's in what was then known as the village, later to disappear into the urban sprawl of Wolverhampton and the West Midlands.

From seemingly hopeless beginnings, Pete carved a niche for himself in music through meeting Steryl Williams and members of the West Indian community, forming one of the earliest and most successful Reggae and Soul outfits in the area. Pete and the band toured extensively until tiredness, fatigue and tragedy struck, leaving him a burned out cinder, with the sounds of mayhem, murder and rioting ringing in his ears.

This book tells the story of these events and the eventual recovery and different road leading into the Folk and Blues clubs in England and Europe.

Pete's early album 'Stay with Shakespear' recorded with Jon Tame is still selling 40 years after their appearance at the Cambridge Folk Festival. With extensive appearances in Europe with Blues legend Gerry Lockran, Pete finished the tour at the Osnabruck Folk and Blues festival.

He then moved on into the Film and Compact Disc Business, working with one of the U.K.'s most successful nightclub owners. Different Roads indeed!

The story of **'Different Roads'** is told using stories, anecdotes, tales of venues, musicians, bands and situations that have passed Pete's way during his sojourn in music. Often we hear of the more famous artistes, but the majority of entertainment shows are performed for the most part by jobbing musicians attempting to make a living. Pete was just one of the thousands throughout the nation who have helped make a night out more special, but with Pete's story you will get a behind the scenes look at the real world of show business, the triumphs and the failures.

'Different Roads' will move you to tears, it will entertain you, it will make you laugh, it may shock you, it will surprise you, but most of all it is hoped that it will encourage you. In what appears to be hopeless situations, with determination and tenacity, ordinary people can do extraordinary things and live to tell the tale!

Enjoy **'Different Roads'**. JH

Printed in Poland
by Amazon Fulfillment
Poland Sp. z o.o., Wrocław